Caxton's
Book of Curtesye.

Early English Text Society.
Extra Series. No. III.
1868

Caxton's
Book of Curtesye,

PRINTED AT WESTMINSTER ABOUT 1477-8 A.D.

AND NOW REPRINTED,

WITH TWO MS. COPIES OF THE SAME TREATISE, FROM
THE ORIEL MS. 79, AND THE BALLIOL MS. 354.

EDITED BY

FREDERICK J. FURNIVALL, M.A.

EDITOR OF 'THE BABEES BOOK, ETC.' ('MANNERS AND MEALS IN OLDEN TIME'),
ETC. ETC.

LONDON:
PUBLISHED FOR THE EARLY ENGLISH TEXT SOCIETY
By HUMPHREY MILFORD, OXFORD UNIVERSITY PRESS,
AMEN HOUSE, E.C.4.
1868 (reprinted 1882, 1898, 1932).

OXFORD
UNIVERSITY PRESS

Great Clarendon Street, Oxford OX2 6DP
United Kingdom

Oxford University Press is a department of the University of Oxford.
It furthers the University's objective of excellence in research, scholarship,
and education by publishing worldwide. Oxford is a registered trade mark of
Oxford University Press in the UK and in certain other countries

© The Early English Text Society 1868

The moral rights of the authors have been asserted

Database right Oxford University Press (maker)

First Edition published in 1868

All rights reserved. No part of this publication may be reproduced,
stored in a retrieval system, or transmitted, in any form or by any means,
without the prior permission in writing of Oxford University Press,
or as expressly permitted by law, or under terms agreed with the appropriate
reprographics rights organization. Enquiries concerning reproduction
outside the scope of the above should be sent to the Rights Department,
Oxford University Press, at the address above

You must not circulate this book in any other form
and you must impose this same condition on any acquirer

Published in the United States of America by Oxford University Press
198 Madison Avenue, New York, NY 10016, United States of America

British Library Cataloguing in Publication Data
Data available

Library of Congress Cataloging in Publication Data
Data available

Extra Series, 3

ISBN 978-0-85-991950-0

PREFACE.

THOUGH no excuse can be needed for including in our Extra Series a reprint of a unique Caxton on a most interesting subject, yet this Book of Curtesye from Hill's MS. was at first intended for our original series, I having forgotten lately that Caxton had written to 'lytyl Iohn,' though some months back I had entered the old printer's book for my second collection of Manners and Meals tracts for the Society. After the copy of Hill—which Mr W. W. King kindly made for his fellow-members—had gone to press, Mr Hazlitt reminded me of the Caxton, and its first and last lines in Mr Blades's admirable book showed that Hill's text was the same as the printed one. I accordingly went to Cambridge to copy it, and there, before tea, Mr Skeat showed me the copy of *The Vision of Piers Plowman* which the Provost and Fellows of Oriel had been good enough to lend him for his edition of 'Text B.' Having enjoyed the vellum Vision, I turned to the paper leaves at its end, and what should they contain but an earlier and better version of the Caxton that I had just copied part of?[1] I drank seven cups of tea, and eat five or six large slices of bread and butter, in honour of the event;[2] and Mr Skeat, with his never-

---

[1] Mr Bradshaw was kind enough to copy the rest, and to read the whole of the proof with Caxton's original.

[2] I must be excused for not having found the poem before, as it is not in the Index to Mr Coxe's Catalogue. In the body of the work it is entered as "A father's advice to his son; with instructions for his behaviour as a king's or nobleman's page. ff. 88, 89, 78. Beg.
Kepeth clene and leseth not youre gere."

THE ORIEL TEXT THE BEST.

failing kindness, undertook to copy and edit the Oriel text for the Society. With three texts, therefore, in hand, I could not well stick them at the end of the Postscript to the *Babees Book*, &c.,[1] and as I wanted Caxton's name to this Book of Curtesye to distinguish it from what has long been to me THE Book of Courtesy,—that from the Sloane MS. 1986, edited by Mr Halliwell for the Percy Society, and by me for our own E. E. T. S.—and as also Caxton's name is one 'to conjure withal,' I have, with our Committee's leave, made this little volume an Extra Series one, and called it Caxton's, though his text is not so good as that of the Oriel MS.

On this latter point Mr Skeat writes:

"The Oriel copy is evidently the best. Not only does it give better readings, but the lines, as a rule, run more smoothly; and it has an extra stanza. This stanza, which is marked 54, occurs between stanzas 53 and 54 of the other copies, and is of some interest and importance. It shows that Lidgate's pupil, put in mind of Lidgate's style by the very mention of his name, introduces a ballad of three stanzas, in which every stanza has a burden after the Lidgate manner. The recurrence of this burden no doubt caused copyists to lose their place, and so the stanza came to be omitted in other copies. Its omission, however, spoils the ballad. Both it and the curious lines in Piers Ploughmans Crede,

For aungells and arcangells · all þei whijt vseþ
And alle aldermen · þat ben *ante tronum*,

i. e. all the elders before the throne, allude to Rev. iv. 10. This Crede passage has special reference to the *Carmelites* or *White* Friars.

"The first two leaves of the Oriel copy are misplaced inside out at the end; but this is not the only misarrangement. The poem has evidently been copied into this MS. from an older copy having a leaf capable of containing *six stanzas at a time;* which leaves were out of order. Hence the poem in the Oriel MS. is written in the following order, as now bound up, Stanzas 11 (l. 5)—18, 25—30, 37—42, 19—24, 49—54, 31—36, 43—48, 55—76, 8—11 (l. 4), 4 (l. 5)—7, 1—4 (l. 4)."

[1] The Treatises in *The Babees Book*, &c., and the Index at the end, should be consulted for parallel and illustrative passages to those in Caxton's text.

As an instance of a word improved by the Oriel text, may be cited the '*brecheles* feste' of Caxton's and Hill's texts, l. 66, and l. 300,

> ffor truste ye well ye shall you not excuse
> ffrom *brecheles feste*, & I may you espye
> Playenge at any game of rebawdrye.—*Hill*, l. 299—301.

Could it be 'profitless,' from A.-Sax. *bréc*, gain, profit; or 'breechless,' a feast of birch for the boy with his breeches off? The latter was evidently meant, but it was a forced construction. The Oriel *byrcheley* set matters right at once.

Another passage I cannot feel sure is set at rest by the Oriel text. Hill's and Caxton's texts, when describing the ill-mannered servant whose ways are to be avoided, say of him, as to his hair, that he is

> Absolon with disheveled heres smale,
> lyke to a prysoner of saynt Malowes,[1]
> a sonny busshe able to the galowes.—*Hill*, l. 462.

For the last line the Oriel MS. reads,

> *a sonny bush myght cause hym to goo louse*,

and Mr Skeat says,—"This is clearly the right reading, of which *galowes* is an unmeaning corruption. The poet is speaking of the *dirty* state of a bad and ill-behaved servant. He is as dirty as a man come out of St Malo's prison; a sunny bush would cause him to go and free himself from minute attendants. A 'sunny bush' probably means no more than a warm nook, inviting one to rest, or to such quiet pursuits as the one indicated. That this is really the reading is shown by the next stanza, wherein the poet apologizes for having spoken too bluntly; he ought to have spoken of such a chase by saying that he goes *a-hawking* or *a-hunting*. Such was the right euphemism required by 'norture.'"

If this is the meaning, we may compare with it the old poet's reproof to the proud man:

---

[1] An allusion to the strong castle built at St Malo's by Anne, Duchess of Bretayne.—Dyce.

Man, of þi schuldres and of þi side
þou miȝte hunti luse and flee:
of such a park i ne hold no pride;
þe dere nis nauȝte þat þou mighte sle.
Early English Poems, ed. F. J. F., 1862, p. 1, l. 5.

and remember that one of the blessings of the early Paradisaical *Land of Cokaygne* is:

Nis þer flei, fle, no lowse,
In cloþ, in toune, bed, no house.
Ib., p. 157, l. 37-8.

We may also compare the following extract about Homer's death from "Pleasant and Delightfull Dialogues in Spanish and English: Profitable to the Learner, and not vnpleasant to any other Reader. By *John Minsheu*, Professor of Languages in London. 1623," p. 47.

"F... a foole with his foolishnesse framed in his owne imagination may giue to a hundred wise men matter to picke out.

"I, So it hapned to the Poet Homer, that as he was with age blinde, and went walking by the sea shoare, & heard certaine Fishermen talking, that at that time were a *lowsing* themselues, and as he asked them, what fish they caught, they vnderstanding that he had meant their lice, they answered, Those that we [1] haue, we seeke for, and those that we [2] haue not wee finde, but as the good Homer could not see what they did, and for this cause could not vnderstand the riddle, it did so grieue his vnderstanding to obtaine the secret of this matter, which was a sufficient griefe to cause his death."

But the subject is not a very pleasant one for discussion, though the occupation alluded to in the Oriel Text must have been one of the pastimes of many people in Early England.

The book itself, *Lytill Johan*, is by a disciple of Lydgate's—see l. 366, p. 36-7—and contains, besides, the usual directions how to dress, how to behave in church, at meals, and when serving at table, a wise man's advice on the books his little Jack should read, the best English poets,—then Gower, Chaucer, Occleve, and Lydgate,— not the Catechism and Latin Grammar. It was very pleasant to come

---

[1] i. Haue in their clothes. i. lice.   [2] i. Haue not in hand.

off the directions not to conveye spetell over the table, or burnish one's bones with one's teeth, to the burst of enthusiasm with which the writer speaks of our old poets. He evidently believed in them with all his heart; and it would have been a good thing for England if our educators since had followed his example. If the time wasted, almost, in Latin and Greek by so many middle-class boys, had been given to Milton and Shakspere, Chaucer and Langland, with a fit amount of natural science, we should have been a nobler nation now than we are. There is no more promising sign of the times than the increased attention paid to English in education now.

But to return to our author. He gives Chaucer the poet's highest gift, Imagination, in these words,

> what ever to say he toke in his entente,
> his langage was so fayer & pertynante,
> yt semeth vnto manys heryng
> *not only the worde, but veryly the thyng.* (l. 343.)

And though the writer has the bad taste to praise Lydgate more than Chaucer, yet we may put this down to his love for his old master, and may rest assured that though the cantankerous Ritson calls the Bury schoolmaster a 'driveling monk,' yet the larking schoolboy who robbed orchards, played truant, and generally raised the devil in his early days (*Forewords to Babees Book*, p. xliv.), retained in later years many of the qualities that draw to a man the boy's bright heart, the disciple's fond regret. We too will therefore hope that old Lydgate's

> sowle be gon
> (To) the sterred paleys above the dappled skye,
> Ther to syng *Sanctus* insessavntly
> Emonge the mvses nyne celestyall,
> Before the hyeste Iubyter of all. (l. 381-5.)

In old age the present poem was composed (st. 60, p. 42-3); 'a lytill newe Instruccion' to a lytle childe, to remove him from vice & make him follow virtue. At his riper age our author promises his boy the surplusage of the treatise (st. 74, p. 50-1); and if a copy of it exists, I hope it will soon fall in our way and get into type, for 'the more the merrier' of these peeps into old boy-life.

SOME QUESTIONS OF GRAMMAR.

On one of the grammatical forms of the Oriel MS., Mr Skeat writes:

"It is curious to observe the forms of the imperative mood plural which occur so frequently throughout the poem in the Oriel copy. The forms ending in *-eth* are about 31 in number, of which 17 are of French, and 14 of A.S. origin. The words in which the ending *-eth* is dropped are 42, of which 18 are of French, and 24 of A.S. origin. The three following French words take *both* forms; *avyse* or *avyseth*, *awayte* or *awayteth*, *wayte* or *wayteth*; and the five following A.S. words, *be* or *beth*, *kepe* or *kepeth*, *knele* or *knelyth*, *loke* or *loketh*, *make* or *maketh*. Thus the poet makes use, on the whole, of one form almost as often as the other (that is, supposing the scribe to have copied correctly), and he no doubt consulted his convenience in taking that one which suited the line best. It is an instance of what followed in almost every case of naturalization, that A.S. inflections were added to the French words quite as freely as to those of native origin. Both the *-eth* and *-e* forms are commonly used without the word *ye*, though *Be ye* occurs in l. 58. In the phrase *avise you* (l. 78), *you* is in the accusative."

Commenting also on l. 71 of Caxton and Hill, Mr Skeat notices how they have individualised the general 'child' of the earlier Oriel text:

"71. Here we find *child* riming to *mylde*. In most other places it is *Johan*. The rime shows that the reading *child* is right, and *Johan* is a later adaptation. The Oriel MS. never uses the word *Johan* at all; it is always *child*."

I may remark also, that on the question lately raised by Mr Bradshaw, 'who before Hampole,[1] or after him, used *you* for the nominative as well as the correct *ye*,' Hill uses both *you* and *ye*, see l. 47, 51, 52, &c., though so far as a hasty search shows, Lydgate, in his Minor Poems at least, uses *ye* only, as do Lord Berners in his *Arthur of Lytil Brytayne*, ab. 1530, the Ormulum, Ancren Riwle, Genesis and Exodus, William of Palerne, Alliterative Poems, Early Metrical Homilies, &c.[2]

[1] *Pricke of Conscience*, p. 127, l. 4659; and p. xvii.
[2] Mr Skeat holds that in the various reading ȝow drieth from the Univ. Coll.

The final *d, f, t,* of Hill's MS., often have a tag to them. As they sometimes occur in places where I judge they must mean nothing, I have neglected them all. Every final *ll* has a line through it, which may mean *e*. Nearly every final *n* and *m* has a curly tail or line over it. This is printed *e* or ñ, though no doubt the tail and line have often no value at all. The curls to the *r*s are printed *e*, because *ther* with the curly *r*, in l. 521, Hill, rimes to *where* of l. 519.

At the end of Caxton's final *d* and *g* is occasionally a crook-backed line, something between the line of beauty and the ordinary knocker. This no doubt represents the final *e* of MSS., and is so printed, as Mr Childs has not the knocker in the fount of type that he uses for the Society's work. Caxton's ñ stands for *un* in the *-aunce, -aunte*, of words from the French. No stops or inverted commas have been put to Caxton's text here, but the stanzas and lines have been numbered, and side-notes added.

"The *Book of Curtesye*," says Mr Bradshaw, "is known from three early editions. The first, without any imprint, but printed at Westminster by Caxton ab. 1477-78,[1] the only known copy of which is here reproduced. The second (with the colophon 'Here endeth a lytyll treatyse called the booke of Curtesye or lytyll John. Emprynted atte Westmoster') is only known from a printer's proof of two pages[2] preserved among the Douce fragments in the Bodleian. It must have been printed by Wynkin de Worde in Caxton's house ab. 1492. In the third edition it was reprinted at the end of the *Stans puer ad Mensam* by Wynkin de Worde ab. 1501-1510. The Cambridge copy is the only one known to remain of this edition."

I have no more to say: but, readers, remember this coming New Year to do more than last for what Dr Stratmann calls "the dear Old English." Think of Chaucer when his glad spring comes, and

---

Oxford MS. (of the early part of the 15th century) to the Vernon MS. þou druiʒest, l. 25, Passus 1, of the Vision of Piers Plowman, the ʒow is an accusative, " exactly equivalent to the Gothic in the following passage—' hwana þaursjai, gaggai du mis, i. e. *whom* it may thirst, let him come to me.' John vii. 37. I conclude that ʒow is accusative, not dative. The same construction occurs in German constantly, '*es dürstet mich* ' = it thirsts me, I thirst."

[1] In his type No. 2, *Blades*, ii. 63.
[2] In Caxton's type No. 5, *Blades*, ii. 235 (not 253 as in Index).

every day besides; forget not Langland or any of our early men:

>   reporte
>   & revyue *the* lawde of the*m* th*a*t were
>   famovs i*n*[1] owr*e* langage, these faders dere,
>   whos sowles i*n* blis, god ete*r*nall avaunce,
>   *th*at lysten so[2] owr*e* langage to enhavnce!
>   (*Hill*, l. 430-4.)

3, *St George's Square, N.W.*
     15 *Dec.*, 1867.

---

[1] Founders of, *Oriel* MS.   [2] some, *Hill;* so, *Oriel.*

The Book of Curtesye.

[The Book of Curtesy.]

[From the Oriel MS. lxxix.]

[1]

Lytle childe, sythen youre tendre infancie
Stondeth as yett vndir yndyff[e]rence,
To vice or vertu to moven [1] or Applie,   3 [1] MS. woorven
And in suche Age ther is no prouidence,
Ne comenly no sadde intelligence,
But ryght as wax receyueth printe and figure,
So chylder ben disposed of nature,

[2]

Vice or vertu to Folowe and ympresse
In mynde; and therfore, to stere and remeve
You from vice, and to vertu thou [2] dresse,   10 [2] Read you
That on to folow, and the other to eschewe,
I haue devysed you this lytill newe
Instruccion according to youre age,
Playne in sentence, but playner in langage.   14

(*Richard Hill's Commonplace Book, or Balliol MS.* 354, *fl C lx.*)

Here begynnyth lytill Iohan.

Lytell Iohan, sith your tendere enfancye   [*Hill's Text*]
Stondyth as yet vndere Indyfference
To vyce or vertu to mevyn or applie,
4 & in suche age *ther* [1] ys no provydence,
Ne comenly no sage Intelygence,
But as wax receyvith prynt or fygure,
So chyldren bene disposed of nature

[1] The *th* is the same as the *y*.

[The Book of Curtesye.]

[Caxton's Text.]

[1]

ytyl Iohn syth your tendre enfancye
Stondeth as yet vnder / in difference
To vice or vertu to meuyn or applye
And in suche age ther is no prouidence
Ne comenly no sade Intelligence
But as waxe resseyueth prynte or figure
So children ben disposide of nature

[Leaf 1 a.]
As Infancy is indifferent whether it follows vice or virtue,

3

7

[2]

Vyce or vertue to folowe ande enpresse
In mynde / ande therfor / to styre & remeue
You from vice / ande to vertue addresse
That one to folowe / and that other teschewe
I haue deuysed you / this lytyl newe
Instruccion / acordynge vnto your age
Playne in sentence / but playner in langage

I have written this new treatise to draw you from vice, and turn you to virtue.

10

14

---

8 ¶ Vyce or vertu to folowe, & enpresse
In mynde; & therfor to styre & remeve
you frome vice, & to vertu addresse,
That on to folow, & that other to eschewe,
12 I haue devysed you this lytitl newe
Instruccion[1] accordyng vnto your age,
playn In sentence, but playnere In langage.

[Hill's Text.]

[1] The mark of contraction is over the *n* : t. i. the *n* has its tail curled over its back like a dog's.

2

[3]

Taketh hede therfore and herkyn what I say,
  And yeueth therto hooly youre aduertence,
Lette not youre eye be here and youre hert away,   17
  But yeueth herto youre besy diligence,
  And ley aparte alle wantawne insolence,
    Lernyth to be vertues and well thewid ;
    Who wolle not lere, nedely must be lewid.   21

[4]

Afore all thyng, fyrst and principally,
  In the morowe when ye¹ shall vppe ryse,   ¹ MS. he.
To wyrship god haue in youre memorie ;   24
  Wyth cristis crosse loke ye blesse you thriese,
  Youre pater-nosteir seyth in devoute wyse,
    Aue maria wyth the holy crede,
    Than alle the after the bettir may ye spede.   28

[5]

And while ye be Abouten honestely
  To dresse youre-self and don on youre aray,
Wyth youre felawe well and tretably   31
  Oure lady matens Avyseth that you say,
  And this obseruaunce vseth euery day,
    Wyth prime and owris, and wythouten drede
    The blyssed lady woll graunte you youre mede.   35

    ¶ Take hede therfor, & harken what I saye,   [Hill's Text.]
16   & geve therto yowre good advertence,
      lette not your ere be here, & your herte awaye,
      But pute you therto besy delygence,
      Laying a-parte all wanton Insolence,
20   lernyd to be vertuvs & well thewed ;
        who will not lerne, nedely he must be lewed.

    ¶ Afore all thyng, & pryncypally
      In the mornyng whan ye vp ryse,
24   To worship god haue in memory ;
        with crystis crosse loke ye blesse ye thryse,

[3]

Take hede therfore / and herkne what I saye
Ande gyue therto / your goode aduertence
Lete not your ere be here & your herte awaye 17
But put ye therto / besy diligence
Leynge aparte al wantown Insolence
Lerneth to be vertuous / and wel thewede
Who wil not lerne / nedely he must be lewed 21

Attend therefore to what I say.

Learn good manners.

[4]

Afore alle thinge / ande principally
In the morenynge / whan ye vp rise
To worshipe gode / haue in memorie 24
With crystes crosse / loke ye blesse you thrise
Your pater noster / saye in deuoute wyse
Aue maria / with the holy crede
Thenne alle the day / the better shal ye spede 28

[Leaf 1 b.]
On rising,

cross yourself,
say your Pater Noster, Ave, and Creed.

[5]

And while that ye be aboute honestly
To dresse your self / & do oñ your araye
With your felawe / wel and tretably 31
Oure lady matyns / loke that ye saye
Ande this obseruañce / vse ye every daye
With pryme and ouris / withouten drede
The blesside lady / wil quyte you your mede 35

While dressing,

say our Lady's Matins,

Prime, and Hours.

[Hill's Text.]

  your patere noster say in devoute wyse,
   Aue maria / with the holy crede ;
28 Then all the day the better shall ye spede.

¶ And while ye dresse your selfe, honestly
  To dresse your selfe & do on your araye,
  with your felowe well & tretably
32 Owre lady matens loke that you say ;
  And this observance vse ye euery day,
  with pryme & owers with-owt drede.
  the blessyd lady will quyte you your mede.

[6]

K embe youre hede and loke ye kepe hit clene,
Youre eris twayne suffre not foule to be;
In youre visage wayteth no spotte be sene, 38
  Purge youre nase, let hit not combred be
  Wyth foule matiers Ayenst all oneste,
    But wyth bare hande no matier from hit feche,
    For that is a foule and an vncurtays teche. 42

[7]

Y oure handes wassheth, that is an holsom thyng,
Youre nayles loke they be not geet blake,
Suffre hem not to ben ouer long growyng; 45
  To youre aray good hede I warne you take,
  That manerly ye seet hit vp and make,
    Youre hode, youre gowne, youre hose, and eke
      youre scho,
    Wyth all array longyng youre body to. 49

[8]

K epeth clene and leseth not youre gere,
And or ye passen oute of youre loggyng,
Euery garment that ye schulle vppon you were, 52
  Awayteth welle that hit be so syttyng
  As to youre degre semeth moost on accordyng;
    Than woll men sey, 'for soth this childe is he
    That is well taught and loueth honeste.' 56

---

36 ¶ Kembe your hede, & loke you kepe yt clene; [*Hill's Text.*]
    your eres twayn suffre not fowle to be; [ffi C lx back]
  In your wysage loke no spote be sene;
    purge your nose; lett no man in yt se
40   The vile matter; yt ys none honeste;
    Ne with your bare hond no fylth from yt feche,
    ffor that ys fowle, & an vncurtoys teche.

  ¶ Your hondis wasshe; yt ys an holsom thyng;
44   your naylis loke they be not gety blake,
    Ne suffre not them over longe growyng.

CAXTON'S TEXT.

[6]

Kembe your hede / & loke ye kepe it clene
Your eres tweyne / suffre not fowl to be
In your visage / wayte no spot be sene   38
Purge your nose / lete noman in it see
The vile mater / it is none honeste
Ne with your bare honde / no filth fro it fecche
For that is fowl / and an vncurtoys teche   42

Comb your head; clean your ears

and nose;

don't pick it.

[7]

Your hondes wesshe / it is an holsom thinge
Your naylis loke / they be not gety blacke
Ne suffre not hem / to be ouer longe growyng   45
To your araye / I warne you good hede take
That manerly ye fytte it vp and make
Your hoode. gowne. hosyn / & eke your sho
With al your aray longyng your body to   49

[Leaf 2 a.] Wash your hands; don't keep your nails jet-black or too long.

Wear fit clothes, that fit well

[8]

Kepe you clene / and lose not your gere
And or ye passe / out of your loggynge
Euery garment / that ye shal on were   52
Awayte wel / that it be so syttynge
As to your degre / semeth acordynge
Thenne wil men saye / forsoth this childe is he
That is wel taught / and louyth honeste   56

and suit your station;

the men will praise you.

[Hill's Text.]

     To your A-raye I warne you good hede take,
     Manerly & ffyte loke you yt make;
48   your hood / gowne / hosen / & eke your sho,
     with all your araye longyng your body to.

¶ Kepe you clene, & lose not your gere;
     & or you passe owt of your lodgyng,
52   Euery garment *that* ye shall were,
     Awayte well *that* yt be so syttyng
     & to your degre semed accordyng;
     Than will men say, "for sothe *th*is child ys he
56   *that* ys well tawght, & loweth honeste."

[9]

And as ye walke and passen be the strete,
Be ye not nyce of chere and countenance;
And loke, my childe, to folkys that ye mete, 59
Ye spekyn feyre wyth wordis of plesaunce;
To youre souerayne wyth humble obeysaunce,
To hym that is youre felowe and pere,
Yevith feyre langage wyth ryght frendly chere. 63

[10]

Cast not wyth stone or styke at foule ne beste,
And where ye walke be ware that ye ne rage,[1]   [1] MS. nerage
For and ye do, ye shall to byrcheley feest. 66
Terre[2] wyth no hounde in fylde nor in village,   [2] MS. There, by mistake.
Gothe forth in peace, demenyng youre vysage
In sobre wyse, that men may of you say,
'A goodly childe ther passith be the way.' 70

[11]

Whan ye come to the chirche, my lytyll chylde,
Holy watir ye schull vppon you caste 72
Be-fore the crosse wyth [chere] moste meke and mylde;
Than knelyth doune and knoketh on youre breste,
Thankyng the lorde that on the crosse did rest,
And there for you suffred his hert to blede,
Seyth or ye ryse Pater, Aue, and A crede. 77

   ¶ And as ye walke & passe by the strete,   [Hill's Text.]
    Be ye not Nyce of chere & covntenavnce,
   but loke, my child, to folkis that you mete,
60   & loke ye speke fayere with wordis of plesavnce,
    Demvre, & curtoys of your Demenavnce.
    To hym that ys yowre felow & pere,
    Geve you fayre langage & a ffrendly chere.

64 ¶ Cast no styke ne stone at fowle ne beste;
    & wher ye walke, be ware ye ne rage,
    ffor yff ye do ye shall to brecheles feest.
    Terre not with hovndis in fyld ne in vilage;

[9]

And as ye walke / and passe by the strete
Be ye not nyce of chere / and countenaunce
But loke my child / to folkes that ye mete   59
Ye speke fayr / with wordes of plesaunce
Demure and curtoys / of your demenaunce
To hym that is your felawe ande pere
Gyue ye fair langage / and a frendly chere   63

As you walk, look pleasantly at folk,

and greet your fellows friendly;

[10]

Caste no styck ne stone at fowle ne beest
And where ye walke / bewarre ye ne rage
For yf ye doo / ye shal to brecheles feest   66
Terre not with hounde in felde ne in vilage
Go forth your waye / demenyng your viage
In sobre wyse / that men may of you saye
A goodly chylde / ther passeth by the waye   70

[Leaf 2 b.] don't shy stones at bird or beast,

or quarrel with dogs.

[11]

And whan ye come to þᵉ chirche my litil child
Holy water / ye shal vpon you caste
Byfore þᵉ crosse / with chere meke & mylde   73
Knele adoun / and knocke on your breste
Thankyng the good lord þᵗ on it dide reste
And there / for you suffryd his sides to blede
Saye ye or ye rise / pater noster / aue / & a crede   77

At church, holy-water yourself,

kneel before the cross, knock on your breast,

and say prayers.

---

68   Go furth your way, Demenyng your viage   [*Hill's Text.*]
      In sober wyse, that men maye of you saye,
      " A goodly chyld ther passith by the way."

¶ And when ye cum to the churche, my litill child,
72   holy water ye shall vpon you caste.
      be-fore the crosse with chere meke & mylde
      knele a-downe, & knoke on your brest,
      Thankyng that good lord that on yt dyde reste,
76   & ther for you suffred his sydys to blede ;
      Saye ye, or you ryse, pater noster / aue / & a crede.

[12]

Avise you well Also for eny thyng,
The schirche of prayer is the house and place,
Be ware there-fore of clappe or Ianglyng,　　　80
  For in the schirche that is full gret trysspace,
  And A token of hem that lacken grace;
    Ther beth demure and kepeth youre sylence,
    And serueth god wyth all youre deligence.　　　84

[13]

TO helpe the prest whan he shall sey the masse,
Whan hit shall happen you or be-tyde,
Remeue not ferre ne from his presence passe,　　　87
  Kneleth or stondeth deuoutly hym be-syde,
  And not to nyghe; youre tounge mooste be applied
    To Answere hym wyth[1] v[o]ice full moderate;　　　[1] MS. wyth hym wyth.
    Avyse you well, my lityll childe, Algate　　　91

[14]

TO mynystre wyth de-voute Reuerence,
Loke that ye do youre humble obseruaunce
Debonarly wyth [dewe] obideence,　　　94
  Cyrcum-spectly, wyth euer[y] circumstaunce
  Of porte, of chere, demevire of countenaunce,
    Remembryng, the lord aboue is he
    Whom to serue is grettest liberte.　　　98

  ¶ Avyce you well also for any thynge,　　　[Hill's Text.]
    The chyrche, of prayer ys howse & place;
80 be ware therfor of clappe or Iangelynge,
    ffor in the chyrche yt ys a full gret trespas,
    & a token of suche as lacketh grace.
    Ther be ye demvre, & kepe ye scilence,
84 And serve ye god with all your delygence.

    To helpe the Preest whan he sayth masse,　　　[ff C lj.]
    whan yt shall happen you or betyde,
    Remeve not fer, ne from his presence passe;
88 knele or stonde you devovtly hym besyde,

CAXTON'S TEXT.

[12]

Auyse you wel also / for ony thinge
The chirche of prayer / is hous and place
Beware therfore / of clappe or Iangelynge   80   Don't chatter,
For in þᵉ chirche / it is a ful grete trespaas
And a token of suche / as lackyth grace
There be ye demure / and kepe ye scilence   but be silent, and serve God.
And serue ye god / with al your diligence   84

[13]

To helpe the preest / whan he saith masse   [Leaf 3 a.] When you help the priest at Mass,
Whan it shal happen you or betyde
Remeue not fer / ne from his presence passe   87
Knele or stonde ye / deuoutly hym besyde   kneel or stand near him,
And not to nygh your tonge muste be applide
Tanswere hym / with voys ful moderate   and answer him in a moderate
Auyse you wel / my lityl childe algate   91   tone.

[14]

To mynystre / with deuoute reuerence   Minister reverently
Loke ye do / youre humble obseruañce
Debonairly / with due obedyence   94
Circumspectly / with euery circumstaunce   and circumspectly.
Of poort and chere / of goodly countenañce
Remembrynge wel the lorde / a boue is he
Whom to serue / is grettest liberte   98

    & not to nygh : your tonge mvst be applyde   [Hill's Text.]
       To answere hym with woyce moderate.
       Avyce you well, my lytill child, algate

92 ¶ To mynyster with devout reverence ;
     loke ye do your humble observaunce
   Debonerly wyth dewe obedyence,
   Circumspectly with euery circumstavnce
96   Of poort, & chere of goodly covntenavnce,
   Remembryng well the lorde a-bove ys he,
   whome to serve ys grettest lyberte.

[15]

And whan ye speke, loketh men in the face [1]   [1] MS. visage.
Wyth sobre chere and goodly semblaunce;
Cast not youre eye asyde in odir place,   101
For that is a tokyn of wantowne inconstaunce,
Which wolle appeyre youre name, and disauaunce;
The wyse man seyth, 'who hathe this signes thre
Ne is not like a good man [for] to be—   105

[16]

Yn hert,' he seyth, 'who that is inconstaunte,[2]   [2] MS. inconstaunce
A waveryng eye, glyddryng but sodenly
From place to place, and A fote[3] variaunte[4]   108   [3] MS. fore. [4] MS. variaunce.
That in no place abydeth stabully—
Thes ben signes,' the wyse man seyth sekerly,
'Of suche a wyght as is vnmanerly nyce,
And is full like dissposed be to vice.'   112

[17]

And wayte, my childe, whan ye stond at the table,
Of souereyne or maister whether hit be,
Applieth you [for] to be seruysable,   115
That no defaute in you may founde be;
Loke who doth best and hym envyeth ye,
And specially vseth attendaunce,
Whiche is to souereyne thyng of gret plesaunce. 119

¶ And whan ye speke, loke men in the face   [Hill's Text.]
100   with sobre chere & goodly semblavnce;
Caste not eye a-side in no othere place,
ffor that ys a token of a wanton constavnce
which will apayre your name, & dysavance.
104   The wyse man sayth, 'who hath these thyngis iij,
ys not lyke a good man for to be:

¶ 'In herte,' he sayth, 'who that ys Inconstavnte,
A waverynge eye, glydyng sodenly
108   ffro place to place, & a foote varyavnte
that in no place a-bydyth stabli,

[15]

And whan ye speke / loke men in the face		When you speak to men, look 'em in the face.
With sobre chere / ande goodly semblaunce		
Caste not your eye a syde / in other place	101	
For that is a token of wantouñ inconstance		
Whiche wil appeyre your name & disauañce		
The wise man saith who hath these thingis thre		The Wise Man says
Is not lyke a goode man for to be	105	

[16]

In herte he seith / who that is inconstañte		[Leaf 3 b.]
A waueryng eye / glydyng sodeynly		an inconstant man with a wavering eye and a wandering foot
Fro place to place / & a foot variañte	108	
That in no place / abydeth stably		
These ben þe signes / the wiseman seith sikerly		
Of suche a wight / as is vnmanerly nyce		
And is ful likely disposid vnto vyce	112	will turn to vice.

[17]

Awayte my chylde / whan ye stande atte table		When you serve at table,
Of maister or souerayn / whether it be		
Applye you for to be seruysable	115	be attentive and redy.
That no defaute in you founden be		
Loke / who doth best / and hym ensiewe ye		
And in especyal / vse ye attendaunce		specially to well-off men.
Wherein ye shal your self best auaunce	119	

    Thyse bene *the* thyng*is*,' *the* wysman sayth sekerly,   [*Hill's Text.*]
      'Off suche a wayghte *that* be vnmanerly nyce,
112   & be fułł lykely dysposed vnto vyce.'

¶ Awayte, my chyld, whan ye stonde at table,
   Off mayster or soverayne whe*ther* yt be,
   Applye you for to be servysable
116 That no defawte in you fownden be ;
   loke who dothe best, & hym folow ye,
   & in especyałł vse ye attendavnce
   wheryn ye shałł your selfe best avaunce.

[18]

A [s] ye be comaundyd, so ye do algate,
Beth not wyth-oute cause from the tabul absent;
Hit is plesaunce vnto the gret astate 122
To se theyre saruaunt about them present;
Haunteth no halkes, for then ye woll be schent.
Lette maner and Mesure be youre guydes twey,
So shall ye best please, I dare well sey. 126

[19]

Rewarde all-way the loke and countenaunce
Of youre master, or of youre souereine,
Ther shall ye best preue what is plesaunce, 129
And what displesaunce; this is the soth serteyne,
The chere discureth often tyme both twayne,
And eke the chere may some tyme you addresse
In thyng that langage may not þan expresse. 133

[20]

And what ye here there, loke ye kepe hit secre,
Besy report of mystrust is cheff norice;
Mekell langage may not all fautles be; 136
Than doth, my childe, as teicheth you the wyse,
Whiche vnto you this wysdome dothe devise,
'Here and see, be still in euery prees,[1]
Passe forth youre way in silence and in pees.'

[1] MS. 'in enery place and in prees.' *Place* was to have been the last word; *and in prees* was carelessly *added*, instead of striking out *place*.—Sk.

---

120 ¶ As ye be comavnded, so do ye algate;   [*Hill's Text.*]
    be not cavseles fro the table absente;
    yt ys a grete pleasure to the high estate [1]   [1 noble, lord.]
      To se his servaunttes abowte hym presente.
124   havnte no halke, for then ye will be shente;
      lette manere & mesure be your gydes twayne;
      so shall ye best please, I dare savely sayne.

   ¶ Reward also thy loke & contenavnce,
128   Off your master or of your soverayne,
     so shall ye best preve what ys his plesavnce
     or ellis his dysplesavnce : this ys sertayne,

[18]

As ye be comandede / so do ye algate
Be not causeles / fro the table absent
It is a grete plesure / to the hyghe estate 122
To see his seruantis aboute hym present
Haunte no halke / for thenne ye wil be shente
Lete maner & mesure / be your gydes tweyne
So shal ye best plese / I dar sauely seyne 126

Don't absent yourself from table,

or stick yourself in a corner. Let Manners and Moderation guide you.

[19]

Rewarde also the loke ande contenaunce
Of your maister / or of your souereyne
So shal ye best preue. what is his plesañce 129
Or els displesaunce / this is soth serteyne
The chere discouerith / often bothe tweyne
And eke þe chere / somtyme may you addresse
In thingis / þ^t langage may not them expresse 133

[Leaf 4 a.] Look at your master's face; that'll show whether he's pleased or not.

[20]

Ande that ye her loke / kepe alway secree
Besy reporte / of mischief is chief noryse
Mykyl langage / may not al fawtles bee 136
Thenne do my childe / as techeth you the wyse
Whiche vnto you / this lesson doth deuyse
Here and see / ande be stylle in euery prees
Passe forth your way in scilence & in pees 140

Keep secret all you hear.

Hear, see, and go your way.

      The chere discovereth oftyn both[e] twayn,
132   & eke the chere sumtyme may yow addresse
      In thyngis the langage may not then expresse.

[Hill's Text.]

¶ And *that* ye here, loke ye kepe alway secre ;
   besy reporte, of myschefe ys chefe noryse ;
136 Mykyll langage may not all fawtles be ;
   Then do, my chyld, as techeth you *the* wyse
   whiche vnto you *this* lessun doth devyce :
   here & see, & be styll in euery prees,
140 passe forthe your way in scilence & in pees.

[fll C lxj, back.]

[21]

And yit in Aventure ye, if the caase require,
Ye most speke as hit may doo percace;[1]   [1] MS. precace.
Seuen condicions obserue as ye shall hire,   143
  Avise you well what ye sey and in what place,
  Of whom, and to whom, in youre mynde compace;
    Howe ye shall speke, and whan, taketh good hede,
    This counseilleth the wyse man wyth-outen drede.

[22]

Awayte, my childe, ye haue you manerly,
Whan at youre mete ye sittyn at youre table;
In euery pres, in euery company,   150
  Disposeth you to be so componable,
  That men may you reporte for comendable;
    For tristeth well, vppon youre bering
    Men woll you blame or yeven you preysing. 154

[23]

And printeth chiefly in youre memorie,
For A principalle poynt of feire norture,
Ye depraue no man absent especially;   157
  Seint Austyn Amonishith wyth besy cure,
  Howe at the table men shull them assure,
    That there escapeth them no suche langage,
    As myght turne other folke to disparage.   161

¶ And yet in aduenture, yf the caas requyre,   [Hill's Text.]
  ye may speke, but ye must percaas
    Seven[1] condycions observe, as ye may here: [1 Six they are at p. 358, *Babees Book*, of the Wise Man.]
144 Avyce ye well what ye say, & in what place,
    Off whom, & to whom, in your mynd compace;
      how ye shall speke, & whan, take good hede:
      this cow[n]syled the wyse man withowten
      drede.

148 A-wayte, my chyld, ye behaue you manerly
    whan at your mete ye sytte at the table;
    In euery prees & In euery cumpany

[21]

And yet in auenture / yf the caas require
Ye may speke / but ye muste thenne percaas
Seuen condicions obserue / as ye may now hyre   143   *If you must speak, observe the seven conditions.*
Auyse you wel / what ye saye / & in what place
Of whom / & to whom in your mynde compace
How ye shal speke / & whan take good hede
This councelith the wise man withoute drede   147

[22]

Awayte my chylde / ye be haue you manerly   *[Leaf 4 b.]*
Whan at your mete / ye sitte at the table   *When you're at meals,*
In euery prees and in euery company   150
Dispose you to be so compenable   *be companionable*
That men may of you reporte for commendable
For trusteth wel / vpon your berynge
Men wil you blame or gyue preysynge   154

[23]

And prynte ye trewly your memorie
For a princypal point of fair noreture
Ye depraue no man absent especyally   157   *and don't run down absent men. St Austin*
Saynt austyn amonessheth with besy cure
How men atte table / shold hem assure
That there escape them / no suche langage
As myght other folke hurte to disparage   161

     Dyspose you to be so cumpenable   *[Hill's Text.]*
152   that men may of you reporte for commendable;
     ffor, trustyth well, vpon your beryng
     Men will you blame or gyve praysyng.

   ¶ And prynte ye truly this in your memorye
156   for a pryncypall poynt of fayer noretvre,
    that ye deprave no man absente specyally.
     Saynt Austyne amonessheth with besy cure,
     howe men att table shulde them assure
160   that ther escape them no suche langage
     As myght hurte or bryng folke to disparage.

[24]

This curteise clarke writeth in ryght this wyse,
Rebukyng the vice of vile detraccioun ;
'What man hit be that of custome and guise   164
Hurteth wyth his toung wyth foule corrosioun
The absent wight, for that abusioun
Suche detractoure [wayue][1] from this table   [1] A word lost.
As vn-worthe, not to be reprocheable.   168

[25]

Whan ye sitten therfor at youre repaste,
Annoyethe no man present nor absent,
But speketh feyre, for and ye make waste   171
Off [large] langage, for soth ye·most be schent ;
And wan ye spcke, speketh wyth good entent
Of maters appendyng to myrth and plesaunce,
But nothyng that may causen men greuaunce.   175

[26]

Eschewe also taches of foule rauenyng,
Of gredy lust the vncurteyce appetite ;
Pres not to sone to youre viaunde, restraine   178
Youre handis a while wyth manerly respytte ;
Fedith for necessite, not for delite,
Demeneth you in mete and drink soo sobrely,
That ye be not infecte wyth gloteny.   182

   ¶ This curteys clerke wryteth in this wyse,   [Hill's Text.]
      Rebukyng the vyce of vyle detraccion :
164 what may yt be that of custum & gvyse
      hurteth with tonge or by fowle colusyou
      The absente / weyne[1] ye for that abusyou   [1] or weyue]
      Suche a detractowre from the table
168 As vnworthy & also reprocheable.

   ¶ Whan ye sytte therfor at your repast,
      Annoye ye no man present nor absente,
      but speke ye fewe ; for yff ye make wast
172 of large langage, for soth ye must be shent.

[24]

This curtoys clerk / writeth in this wise
Rebukynge the vice / of vyle detraccion *rebukes the vice of detraction,*
What man it be / that of custom & guyse 164
Hurteth with tunge / or by foule colusiōn *and bids you turn all backbiters from the table*
Thabsente / weyue ye for that abusioñ
Suche a detractour / from the table
As vnworthy / and also reprochable 168

[25]

Whan ye sitte therfore at your repaste *[Leaf 5 a.]*
Annoye ye noman presente nor absente
But speke ye fewe / for yf ye make waste 171 *Speak little,*
Of large langage / for sothe ye must be shent
And whan ye speke / speke ye with good entent *and that pleasantly.*
Of maters acordynge vnto plesance
But nothing / that may cause men greuañce 175

[26]

Eschewe also tacches of foule Raueyne *Don't be ravenous,*
Of gredy luste / with vncurteys appetyte [1]
Prece not to sone / fro your viand restreyne 178 *but keep your hands from your food for a time.*
Your honde a while / with manerly respite
Fede you for necessite / & not for delite
Demene you with mete / & drynke so sobrely
That ye not ben enfecte with glotony 182

[1] *Orig.* appetyce.

& whan ye speke // speke with good Intent *[Hill's Text.]*
Off maters accordyng vnto plesavnce,
but no thynge that may cavse men grevaunce.

¶ Eschewe also tacches of fowle ravayne,
177 of gredy luste; with vncurteys appetyte
prece not to sone; fro your vyande restrayne
your hand a while with manerly respyte;
180 ffede you for necessyte, & not for delyte.
Demene you with mete & drynke so soberly
That ye not be Infecte wyth glotony.

[27]

Embrewe not youre vesselle ne youre cuppe [1]
  Ouer mesure and maner, but saue them clene;
Ensoyle not youre cuppe, but kepe hit clenely,   185
  Lete no fatte ferthyng of youre lippe be sen.
  For that is foule; wotte you what I mene?
    Or than ye drincke, for youre owne honeste,
    Youre lippis wepe, and klenly loke they be.   189

[1] *Sic.* Read "napery."

[28]

Blowe not in youre drincke ne in youre potage,
  Ne farsith not youre disshe to full of brede,
Ne bere not youre knyf towarde youre vysage,   192
  For there-in is parell and mekell drede.
  Clawe not youre face ne touche not youre hede
    Wyth youre bare hande, sittyng at the table,
    For in norture that is reprouable.   196

[29]

Lowse not youre gyrdyll syttyng at youre table,[2]
  For that is a tache of vncurtesye,
But and ye seme ye be enbrasyde streite,   199
  Or than ye sitte amende hit secrely,
  So couertly that no wyght hit espie.
    Be ware also no breth from you rebounde
    Vppe ne downe, be ware that shamefull sounde.

[2] *Sic.* Read "mete."

¶ Enbrewe not your vessell ne your naprye   [*Hill's Text.*]
184   over maner & mesure, but kepe them clene;   [ffl C lxij.]
  Ensoyle not your cuppe, but kepe yt clenly,
    lete no farsyone on your lyppis be sene,
    ffor that ys fowle; ye wott what I mene.
188   Or than ye drynke, for your own honeste
    your lyppys wype, & clenly loke they be.

¶ Blowe not in your drynke ne in your pottage.
  Ne ferce not your disshe to full of brede;
192 bere not your knyf toward your vysage,
  ffor theryn ys peryll & mykell drede;

[27]

Enbrewe not your vessel / ne your naprye
Ouer maner & mesure / but kepe hem clene
Ensoyle not your cuppe / but kepe it clenlye   185
Lete no fat farssine / on your lippes be sene
For that is fowle / ye wote what I mene
Or than ye drynke / for your owen honeste
Your lippes wype / and clenly loke they be   189

Don't dirty your cloth or cup.

Wipe your lips before you drink.

[28]

Blowe not in your drinke ne in your potage
Ne farse not your dishe to ful of brede
Bere not your knyf / to warde your visage   192
For therin is parelle / and mykyl drede
Clawe not your visage / touche not your hede
With your bare honde / sittyng atte table
For in norture / suche thing is reprouable   196

[Leaf b b.] Don't blow on your food, or put your knife to your face, or scratch it or your head.

[29]

Lose not your gyrdel / sittyng at your mete
For that is a tacche / of vncurtesye
But yf ye seme / ye be embraced streite   199
Or then ye sytte / amende it secretly
So couertly that no wight you espye
Beware also / no breth fro you rebounde
Vp ne douñ / leste ye were shameful founde   203

Don't undo your girdle at table; if it's tight, let it out before you sit down.

Don't break wind up or down.

[Hill's Text.]

196   Clawe not your visage, tovche not your hede
　　　　with your bare honde syttyng at the table,
　　　　ffor in norture suche thyngis be reproveable.

¶ Lose not your gyrdyll syttyng at your mete,
　　ffor that is a tache of vncurtesye ;
　　but yff ye seme ye be enbrased streyte,
200　or than ye sytte, amend yt secretly
　　So wysely that no wyght you aspye.
　　be ware also no breth fro you rebownd
　　Vp ne downe, lest ye were shamfull fownd.

[30]

Beth huste in chambre, cilent in the halle,
  Herkenyth well, yueth good audience;
Yef vsher or marchall for eny romour calle,   206
  Putting Ianglers to rebuke and cilence,
  Beth mylde of langage, demure of eloquence;
    Enforcith you to them confourmyde be,
    That can most good and haue humanyte.   210

[31]

Touche not wyth mete salt in the saler,
  Lest folke Appoynt you of vncunnyngnesse,
Drosse hit apparte vppon a clene tranchere;   213
  Force not youre mouth to fulle for wantannesse,
  Lene not vppon the table, that is but rudesse,
    And yf I shall to you so playnly say,
    Ouer the table ye shull not spette convey   217

[32]

Yif ye be seruid wyth metis delicate,
  Departith wyth youre fellowys in gentyl wyse,
The clarke seith, 'nature is content and saciate   220
  Wyth meane diete, and lytill shall suffice.'
  Departyth therfore, as I to you devise;
    Engrosith not vnto youre silven all,
    For gentilnesse will ay be lyberall.   224

¶ Be ye husht in chambre, scylente in hall;   [*Hill's Text.*]
205   herkyn well, & geve good audyence
     yff vsshar or marchall for any rvmowre call;
     putt ye yanglers to rebuke for scilence.
208   Be ye myld of langage, demvre of eloquence;
     Enforce you vnto hym conformed to be
     that can most good, & hathe humanyte.

¶ Towch not with your mete salte in the saler,
212   leest folke apoynte you of vnconnyngnesse;
     Dresse yt aparte vpon a clene trenshere.
     ffarste not your movth to full for wantonesse;

[30]

Be ye husht in chambre / scylent in halle
Herken wel ande gyue goode audience
Yf vssher or marchal for ony Rumour calle — 206
Put ye Ianglers to rebuke for silence
Be ye mylde of langage / demure of eloquence
Enforce you vnto hym conformed to be
That can moste good / ande hath humanyte — 210

Be silent, and put chatterers to rebuke.

Imitate him who has humanity.

[31]

Touche not with your mete / salt in the saler
Lest folk apoynte you of vnconnyngnesse
Dresse it aparte / vpon a clene trencher — 213
Farse not your mouth to ful / for wantonesse
Lene not vpon the table / for that rude is
And yf I shal to you playnly saye
Ouer the table / ye shal not spetel conueye — 217

[Leaf 6 a.] Don't dip your meat in the saltcellar,

lean on the table,

or spit over it.

[32]

Yef ye be serued / with metes delicate
Departe with your felowe / in gentil wise
The clerck saith / nature is content & saciate — 220
With mene diete / and litil shall suffyse
Departe therfore / as I you deuyse
Engrose not / vnto your self alle
For gentilnes / wil aye be liberalle — 224

Share dainties with your fellows:

gentleness is liberal.

---

216   lene not on the table, for that rvde ys ;
    &yff I shall to you playnly saye,
    over the table ye shall not spetell conveye.

¶ Yff ye be servede with metis delycate,
   Departe with your felawe in gentill wyse ;
220   the clerke seyth, 'nature ys content & sacyate
   with mene dyete, & lytill shall suffyce ;'
   Departe therfor, as I you devyce,
    Engrose not vnto yowre selfe all,
224   ffor gentylnesse will ay be lyberall.

[Hill's Text.]

[33]

And wan percace youre seruice is not large,
Grucchith not wyth frownyng countenaunce,
Ne maketh not ther-of to mekell charge,   227
  Disposeth you to goodly sufferaunce,
  And what ye haue, take hit for suffisaunce ;
    Holde you pleased wyth that god hath you sent,
    He hath Inough[1] that can hold hym content. 231   [1] MS. Inought.

[34]

Burnysh no bonys wyth youre tethe, be ware,
That houndis tecche fayleth of curtesie ;
But wyth youre knyff make the bonys bare ;   234
  Handell youre mete so well and so clenly,
  That ye offenden not the company
    Where ye be sette, as ferre-forth as ye can ;
    Remembre well that maner maketh man.   238

[35]

And whan your teeth shall cutte youre mete small,
Wyth open mouth be ware that ye not ete,
But loke youre lippis be closede as a wall,   241
  Whan to &[2] fro ye trauers youre mete ;   [2] MS. a.
  Kepe you so close that men haue no conceite
    To seyn of you language of vilonye,
    Be cause ye ete youre mete vnma[ne]rly.   245

¶ And whan percaas your servyce ys not large,   [Hill's Text.]
    Groge not with frownynge covntenavnce,
    Ne make ther-of not to mykytt charge ;
228 Dyspose you to goodly suffravnce,
    & what ye haue, take yt in suffysavnce ;
      be you plesid with suche as god hath you sent ;
      he hath ynowgh þat can hold hym contente.

232 Burnysshe no bonys with your teth, be ware,   [ff C lxlj back.]
    Suche howndis tacches fallen of vncurtesye,
    but with your knyfe make the bonys bare.
    Handle your mete so well & so clenly

[33]

And whan percaas your seruise is not large   *If your helping is not large, don't grumble,*
Gruccheth not / with frownyng contenaunce
Ne make therof / not to mykyl charge   227
Dispose you to goodly suffraunce
And what ye haue / take it in suffysaunce
Be ye plesid with suche as god hath you sent   *but be content.*
He hath ynough / that can holde hym content   231

[34]

Burnysshe no bones / with your teth / beware   *[Leaf 6 b.] Don't burnish bones with your teeth.*
Suche houndis tacches / falle of vncurtesye
But with your knyf / make the bones bare   234
Handle your mete / so wel and so clenly   *Handle your food cleanly,*
That ye offende not the company
Where ye be sette / as ferforth as ye can
Remembryng wel / that manners make man   238   *for Manners make Man.*

[35]

Ande whan that / ye ete your mete smalle
With open mouth / beware ye not ete   *Eat with your lips closed*
But loke your lippes / be closed as a walle   241
Whan to ande fro / ye trauerse your mete
Kepe you so cloos / that men haue no conseite
To say of you / ony langage or vilonye
Bicause ye ete your mete / vnmanerly   245

                                                                                                               [Hill's Text.]

236   That ye offende not the company
       wher ye be sette, as ferforthe as ye can,
       Remembryng well that maners make man.

      ¶ And whan that ye ete your mete small,
240   with open mowth be ware ye not ete,
       but loke / your lyppes be closed as a wall ;
       whan to & fro ye traverse your mete,
       kepe you so cloos that men haue no conceyte
244   To saye of you any langage or vylonye
       by cavse ye ete your mete so vnmanerly.

[36]

Be ware, my child, of laughing ou*er* mesure,
  Ye shall not Also at the borde youre naylis pare,
Ne pike not youre teth wyth youre knyff, I you ensure,
    Ete at youre messe, and odir folkes spare ;   249
    A glottou*n* can but make dissches bare,
      And of Inough he taketh neu*er* hede,
      He fedith for lust more than [1] he doth for nede.   [1] MS. that.

[37]

And whan the borde is then [as] of *ser*uice,   253
  Not replenyshide wyth gret diuercite,
Of mete and drincke good chere may than suffice,
    Hit is A signe of gret humanite,   256
    Wyth gladsom chere than fulsom for to be ;
      The poet seyth howe that the poure borde
      Men may encrese wyth cherefull wille and worde.

[38]

And o thing, my childe, I warne you vndirstonde,
  Specially for youre owne honeste,
In the water wasschith so clene youre hande,   262
    That youre towell neuer ensoyled be
    So foule that hit be lothely vnto se ;
      Wasschith wyth watire till youre handis be clene,
      And in youre clothe ther shall no spotte be sene.

¶ Beware, my chyld, of laughynge ou*er* mesure ;   [*Hill's Text.*]
  Ne at *th*e borde ye sha*ll* no nayles pare,
248   Ne pyke yo*ur* teth wi*th* knyf, I you ensure.
  Ete at yo*ur* messe, & othe*r*e folk*is* spare ;
  A gloton ca*n* but make *th*e bonys bare,
  & of ynowgh he takyth nevere hede,
252   he ffedyth more for lust than for nede.

¶ And wha*n* *th*e borde ys thyn as of *ser*vyce,
  Nowght replenysshed wi*th* gret dyversite
  of mete & drynke, gud chere may than suffice,
256   wi*th* honest talkyng ; & also owght ye

[36]

Beware my childe / of laughyng ou*er* mesure	
Ne at the borde / ye shall no naylis pare	Don't pare your nails at table, or
Ne pyke your teth / with knyf / I you ensure 248	pick your teeth with a knife.
Ete at your messe / and other folkes spare	
A gloton can but make the bones bare	
And*e* of ynough / he taketh neuer hede	
He fedith more for lust / than for nede 252	

[37]

And whan þ*e* borde is thynne / as of seruyse	[Leaf 7 *a*.] When there are not many dishes,
Nought replenesshed with grete diuersite	
Of mete & drinke good chere may then suffise 255	be satisfied with chatting cheerily.
With honest talkyng / and also ought ye	
With gladsom chere / thenne fulsom for to be	
The poete saith / hou that a poure borde	
Men may enriche / with cheerful wil & worde 259	

[38]

And one thyng my chylde / ye vnderstonde	
In especyall*e* / for your owne honeste	
In the water / wasshe so clene your honde 262	Wash your hands clean in the water,
That your towel / neuer enfoyled be	so as to leave no dirt on your towel.
So fowle / that it be lothsom on to see	
Wasshe with water / your hondes so cleene	
That in the towel shal no spotte be sene 266	

---

	wi*th* gladsu*m* chere the*n* fulsome for to be :	[*Hill's Text.*]
	The poete seyth how *that* ' a powre borde	
259	Men may enryche wi*th* cherfull will & worde.'	

¶ And on thyng, my child, ye vnderstond,
   In especyall for your own honeste :
   In *the* water wasshe so clene yo*ur* hond
   that your towell never ensoyled be
264 So fowle *that* yt be lothsome on to see ;
   wasshe wi*th* water yo*ur* hond*is* so clene
   that in *th*e towell shall no spote be sene.

[39]

Leue not youre spone in youre dissche standyng,
 Ne vppon the brede hit shall not lie ;
Lette youre trenchoure be clene for eny thyng,   269
 Yif ye haue no chaunge, yit as honestly
 As ye can, maketh avoydie,
  So that no fragment from youre trenchoure falle ;
  Do this, my childe, in chambre and in halle.   273

[40]

Whan Another speketh at the table,
 Be ware ye interrupte[1] not is tale nor langage,
For that is a thing discommendable,   276
 And hit is no signe of folkes sage
 To ben of wordis besy and outrage ;
  For the wyse man seyth pleinly in sentence,
  'He shall be wyse that yevith Audience.'   280

[1] MS. *corruptly* has nattiripte.

[41]

Vndre-stondeth ther-fore or than ye speke,
 Printyng in youre mynde clerely the sentence,
He that vseth A mannes tale to breke   283
 Lettyth vncurtesly the Audience,
 And hurtyth hym-sylf for lacke of silence ;
  He may not yeue answere convenyent
  That herith not fynally what is ment.   287

[*Harl's Text.*]

¶ lete not your spone in youre disshe stond,
268 Ne vpon the table yt shuld not lye ;
  lete your trenchowre be clene for any thyng,
   & yf ye haue, change yet as honestly
   As ye can ; make avoyde manerly
272   So that no fragment fro your trenchere fall :
    Do thus, my child, in chambere & in hall.

 ¶ And whan a-nother man spekyth at the table,
   be ware ye interrupte not his langage,
276 for that ys a thyng on-comendable,
   & yt ys not no signe of folkis sage

CAXTON'S TEXT.

[39]

Lete not your spone / in your disshe stonding
Ne vpon the table / it shold not lye
Lete your trenchour / be clene for ony thing   269
And yf ye haue chañge / yet as honestly
As ye can / make a voyde manerly
So that no fragment / fro your trencher falle
Do thus my childe / in chambre & in halle   273

Don't leave your spoon in your dish or on the table. Keep your trencher clean.

[40]

And whan another man / spekith atte table
Beware ye enterrupte not / his langage
For that is a thinge discomendable   276
Ande it is no signe of folkes sage
To be of langage / besy ande outrage
For the wyse man saide / in his sentence
He sholde be wyse / that gyueth audience   280

[Leaf 7 b.] Don't interrupt man in his talk

[41]

Vnderstonde therfore or than ye speke
Prynte in your mynde / clerly the sentence
Who that vsith / a mannes tale to breke   283
Letteth vncurteysly / alle the audyence
Ande hurteth hym self / for lack of science
He may not gyue answere conuenyente
That herith not fynally / what is mente   287

      To be of langage besy & owtrage ;
      ffor the wyse sayd in his sentence
280   'he shuld be hold [& be wyse]¹ that gevyth
      audyence.'

[Hill's Text.]
[¹ In a later hand, above the line.]

¶ Vnderstond therfor or than ye speke ;
    prynt in your mynde clerly the sentence ;
    who that vsyth a manys tale to breke,
284   lettyth vncurteysly all the audyence
    And hurteth hym self for lake of scyence ;
    he maye not geve answere conuenyente
    that heryth not fynally what ys mente.

[M C lxiij.]

[42]

Be ware Also, my childe, of rehersaille
Of materis whiche ben at the table mevide;
Hit grevith ofte and dothe men disavaylle,   290
  Full many a man that vice hath mysschevide,
  Of evill thyng saide is wors often contrivide;
    Suche reportis alway loke ye esschewe,
    As may of olde frendis make enemyes newe.   294

[43]

Avise you well whan ye take youre disporte,
  Honest games that ye haunte and vse,
And suche as ben of violente reporte,   297
  I counsell you, my childe, that ye refuse;
  For trustith well ye shall nout you excuse
    From berchely fest, yef I may you aspie
    Playng at [1] eny game of rebaudie.   301   [1 MS. or.

[44]

Itt is to A goodly childe well syttyng,
  To vse disportis of myrth and plesaunce,
To harpe and lute, or lustely to syng,   304
  And in the pres ryght manerly to daunce;
  When men se A childe of suche gouernaunce,
    They seyn, 'gladde may this [childes] frendis be
    To haue a sone soo manerly as he.'   308

¶ But beware, my child, also of rehersayle   [Hill's Text.]
289   Off maters whiche be at the table meved;
    It greweth [1] ofte, & doth men dysavayle;   [1 The line is over the th.]
    ffull many a man that vyce hathe myscheved;
292   Off evyll thynke sayd, ys worse contryved;
      Suche reportes alwaye, my child, eschewe,
      As may of olde frendis make enmyes newe.

¶ Avyse you well whan ye take your dysporte,
296   honeste games that ye hawnt & vse;
    & suche as bene of vyleyns report,
      I cownsell you, my child, that ye refuse;

[42]

But beware my childe / also of rehersaylle
Of maters / whiche ben atte table meuide   290
It greuith ofte / ande doth men disauayle
Ful many a man / þᵗ vice hath myscheuide
Of euyl thinge saide / is werse contryuide
Suche reportis / alway my childe eschewe
As may of olde frendis / make enemyes newe   294

Don't repeat what you hear at table.

[43]

Aduise you wel whan ye take your disporte
Honest games / that ye haunte ande vse
And suche as ben of vylayns reporte   297
I counceyl you my chyld / that ye refuse
For truste ye wel / ye shal you not excuse
From brecheles feste / and I may you espye
Playnge at ony game of Rybawdrye   301

[Leaf 8 a.] Play only at proper games.

[44]

It is to a godly chyld wel syttynge
To vse disportes of myrthe & plesañce
To harpe or lute / or lustely to synge   304
Or in the prees right manerly to daunce
Whan men se a chyld of suche gouernance
They saye / glad may this chyldis frendys be
To haue a chylde / so manerly as is he   308

You should harp, lute, sing, or dance.

[Hill's Text.]

300   ffor truste ye well ye shall you not excuse
        ffrom brecheles feste, & I may you espye
        Playenge at any game of rebawdrye.

¶ Ytt ys to a goodly child well syttyng
        To vse dysportes of myrth & plesavnce,
304   to harpe, to lute, or lustyly to synge,
        Or in the prees right manerly to davnce.
        whan men se a child of suche governavnce,
        thei saye, 'glade may this childis frendys be
308   To haue a child so manerly as ys he.'

[45]

Exersice youre-selfe also in redyng
Of bokys enournede wyth eloquence;
Ther shall ye fynde both plesaunce and lernyng,   311
And so ye may in eu*er*y good presence
Some [what] fynde and see as in sentence,
That shall accorde the tyme to ocupie,
That ye not nede to stondyn idelie.   315

[46]

Itt[1] is fare to be cominycatyfe
In matires vnto purpoos according,
So that a wight sume not excessyfe,   318
For trusteth well, hit is tedious thyng
For to here a childe multiplie talkyng,
Yif hit be not to the purpose applied,
And also wyth goodly termys aleyde.   322

[1 MS. lls]

[47]

Redith Gower in his writyng moralle,
That auñcient faders memorie,
Redith his bokis clepide 'confessionalle,'   325
Wyth many anodir vertuous tretie,
Full of sentence sette so frutuously,
That them to rede shall yeue you corage,
So is he fulle of sentence and langage.   329

¶ Excersyse also yo*ur* selfe in redyng   [*Hill's Text.*]
Off bokes enorned wit*h* eloquence,
ther sha*ll* ye fynde bot*h* plesyre & lernynge,
312   so*mwh*at ye may in eu*er*y good presence
Some-what fynde as in sentence
*t*hat sha*ll* accorde the tyme to occupye,
That ye not nede to stonde ydellye.

¶ It ys fayer to be comynycatyfe
317   In maters vnto purpose accordyng,
So *that* a wyghte seme exersyfe;
ffor trustyth we*ll* y*t* ys a tedyovs thy*n*g

[45]

Excersise your self also in redynge		Practise reading of eloquent books.
Of bookes enornede with eloquence		
Ther shal ye fynde / bothe plesir & lernynge	311	
So that ye may / in euery good presence		
Somwhat fynde / as in sentence		
That shal acorde / the tyme to ocupy		
That ye not nede / to stonden ydelly	315	

[46]

It is fayr / for to be comynycatyf		[Leaf 8 b.] It is right to talk pertinently,
In maters vnto purpose acordynge		
So that a wyght seme excersyf	318	
For trusteth wel / it is a tedyous thynge		
For to here a chylde / multeplye talkyng		but a bore if the talk is irrelevant.
Yf it be not to the purpose applyede		
Ande also with / goodly termys alyede	322	

[47]

Redeth gower in his wrytynge moralle		Read Gower's
That auncyent [1] fader of memorye		1 Orig. anucyent.
Redeth his bookes / callede confessionalle	325	*Confessio Amentis,*
With many another vertuous trayttye		
Ful of sentence / set ful fructuosly		
That hym to rede / shal gyue you corage		
He is so ful of fruyt. sentence and langage	329	

320	ffor to here a child multyply talkyng	[Hill's Text.]
	yf yt be not to *th*e purpose applyed,	
	& also wi*th* goodly termes alyed.	
	¶ Redyth gover i*n* his wrytyng moral̄l,	
324	That Auncyente ffader of memorye,	
	Redyth his bookes called co*n*fessyonal̄l,	
	wi*th* many a-nothere vertuvs tretye	
	ful̄l of sentence sett ful̄l fructuously,	
328	That hy*m* to rede shal̄l geve you covrage,	
	he ys so ful̄l of frute, se*n*tence, & langage.	

[48]

O Fader and Founder of eternate eloquence,
That eluminede all this oure britaigne ;
To sone we lost his lauriate presence, 332
O lusty licoure of that fulsome fountaigne ;
Cursed deth, why hast thou this poete slayne,
I mene Fadir chaucers, mastir Galfride?
Allas! the while, that euer he from vs diede. 336

[49]

Redith his bokys fulle of all plesaunce,
Clere in sentence, in longage excellent,
Brefly to wryte suche was his suffesaunce, 339
What-euer to sey he toke in his entent,
His longage was so feyre and pertinent,
That semed vnto mennys heryng,
Not[1] only the worde, but verrely the thing. 343

[1] MS. But.

[50]

Redith, my child, redith his warkys all,
Refuseth non, they ben expedient ;
Sentence or langage, or both, fynde ye shall 346
Full delectable, for that fader ment
Of all his purpos and his hole entent
Howe to plese in euery audience,
And in oure toung was well of eloquence. 350

¶ O fader & fownder of ornate eloquence [Hill's Text.]
   that Illumyned hast all owre bretayne ! [ff C lxiij back.]
332 To sone we loste thy lavreat science,
   O lusty lyqvovre of that fulsum fontayne !
   O cursed deth ! why hast thou that poete slayne,
   I mene fader chavucer, mayster galfryde ?
336 Alas the while that ever he from vs dyed !

¶ Redyth his werkes full of plesavnce,
   Clere in sentence, In langage excellente :
   Bryefly to wryte, such was his suffysavnce,
340 What-evere to say he toke in his entente,

[48]

O fader and founder of ornate eloquence
That enlumened hast alle our bretayne
To soone we loste / thy laureate scyence 332
O lusty lyquour / of that fulsom fontayne
O cursid deth / why hast thou þ{t} poete slayne
I mene fader chaucer / maister galfryde
Alas the whyle / that euer he from vs dyde 336

and the Father and Founder of Eloquence, [Leaf 163, back.]

mayster Galfryde Chawcer,

[49]

Redith his werkis / ful of plesaunce
Clere in sentence / in langage excellent
Briefly to wryte / suche was his suffysañce 339
What euer to saye / he toke in his entente
His langage was so fayr and pertynente
It semeth vnto mannys heerynge
Not only the worde / but verely the thynge 343

[Leaf 9 a.] whose works are full of pleasaunce,

whose language seems not only words, but truly things.

[50]

Redeth my chylde / redeth his bookes alle
Refuseth none / they ben expedyente
Sentence or langage / or bothe fynde ye shalle 346
Ful delectable / for that good fader mente
Of al his purpose / and his hole entente
How to plese in euery audyence
And in our tunge / was welle of eloquence 350

Read all his books; refuse none:

he is delightful.

[Hill's Text.]

343   his langage was so fayere & pertynente,
     yt semeth vnto manys heryng
    Not only the worde, but veryly the thyng.

¶ Redyth, my child, redyth his bookes all,
   Refusith Non, they ben expedyente ;
  sentence or langage, both fynd ye shall ;
  full delectable that good fader mente,
348   for all his purpose & his hole entente
    [was] how to please in euery audyence,
     & In owre tonge was well of Eloquence.

[51]

Beholde Oclyff in his translacion,
In goodly langage and sentence passing wyse,
Yevyng the prince suche exortacion 353
  As to his highnesse he coude best devyse.
  Of trouth, peace, of mercy, and of Iustice,
    And odir vertuys, sparing for no slouthe
    To don his devere, and quiten hym, as trouth 357

[52]

Required hym, anenste his souereyne,
Most dradde and louyd, whos excellent highnesse
He aduertysede by his writing playne, 360
  To vertue perteynyng to the nobles
  Of a prince, and berith wyttenesse
    His trety entitlede ' of regyment,'
    Compyled of most entier true entent. 364

[53]

Loketh Also vppon dan Iohn lidgate,
My mastire, whilome clepid monke of bury,
Worthy to be renownede laureate, 367
  I pray to gode, in blis his soule be mery,
  Synging ' Rex Splendens,' the heuenly ' kery,'
    Among the muses ix celestiall,
    Afore the hieghest Iubiter of all. 371

¶ Behold Ocklyf in his transslacion,[1]   [*Harl's Text.*]
352 In goodly langage & sentence passyng wyse   [1 transflacion]
    howe he gewyth his prince such exortacion
    As to the hyeste he covld best devyse
    Off trowth / pees / mercy / & Iustyse,
356 & vertu, lettyng for no slowth
    To do his devoyre & qvyte hym his trowth.

¶ Requyre hym As Agaynst his soverayne,
    moste Drade & loved, whose excellent hyenes
360 he advertysed by his wrytyng playne
    To vertu aperteynyng to nobles

[51]

Beholde Ocklyf in his translacion *Read Occlevetoo,*
In goodly langage / & sentence passyng wyse
How he gyueth his prynce / suche exortacion   353 *who gave his Prince such wise advice*
As to the hyest / he coude best deuyse
Of trouthe. pees. mercy. and Iustise
And vertues / leetyng for no slouthe
To do his deuoir & quite him of his trouthe   357

[52]

Requirede hym / as ayenst his souerayne *[Leaf 9 b.]*
Most drade & louyde / wos excellent hyeues
He aduertysede / by his wrytynge playne   360
To vertu / apperteynyng to nobles
Of a prynce / as bereth goode witnes
His traytye / entitlede of regymente *in his treatise De Regimine*
Compylede of entyer trewe entente   364 *Principum.*

[53]

Loke also / vpon dan Iohn lydgate *John Lydgate, too, my master.*
My maister whylome / monke of berye
Worthy to be renomede / as poete laureate   367
I praye to gode in blysse his soule be mercy *(I pray God his soul is singing Rex splendens*
Syngynge Rex splendens that heuenly kyrye
Amonge the muses nyne celestyalle
Byfore the hyest Iubyter of alle   371

[Hill's Text.]

  Off a prince, as beryth god wytnes,
   hys treatye entytled of regemente,
364 Compyled of entyer trewe entente.

  ¶ Loke also than vpon Iohan lydgate,
   My mayrster, whylom monke of bury,
   worthy to be renomed As poete lavreate ;
368 I pray to god in blysse his sowle be mery,
   Syngyng / Rex splendens / that hevenly Kyrye,
   Amonge the mvses nyne celestyall
   be-fore the hyghest Iubyter of all,

[54]

I not why deth my mastir*e* dide envie,
But for he shuld*e* chaunge his habite ;
Pety hit is that suche a man shulde die ! 374
  But nowe I trist he be a carmylite ;
  His amyse blacke is chaunged into white,
    Among the muses ix celestiall,
    Afore the hieghest Iubiter of all ; 378

[55]

Passing the muses all of elicon*e*,
Where is ynympariable of Armonye,
Thedir I trist my mastir-is soule is gon*e*, 381
  The sterr*e*de palays aboue dapplede skye,
  Ther to syng 'sanctus' incessantly
    Among the muses ix celestiall,
    Affore the highest Iubiter of all. 385

[56]

Redith is volumes that ben so large and wyde,
Souereynly sitte in sadnesse of sentence,
Elumynede wyth colouris fresshe on eu*ery* syde, 388
  Hit passith my wytte, I haue no eloquence
  To yeue hym lawde aftir his excellen*c*e,
    For I dare say he lefte hym not on lyue,
    That coude his cu*n*nyng suffisantly discreue. 392

---

372   [Omitted. See Preface, p. ii.]   [*Hill's Text.*]

376

  ¶ Passyng the mvses nyne of elycon,
380   Wher ys no pareyll of Armonye ;
    Thyder I trust my Maysters sowle be gon,
    The sterred paleys above *the* dappled skye,

CAXTON'S TEXT.

[54]

[Omitted. See Preface, p. ii.]

374

378

[55]

Passynge the muses nyne of Elycoñ
Where is non pareyl of armonye
Thider I truste my meistres soule begone   381   in the starred
The sterride paleys / aboue the dapplyd skye   palace above the
                                                    dappled sky,
There to synge sanctus incessantly   before the
Amonge the muses ix celestyalle
Byfore the hyest / Iubiter of alle   385   highest
                                                    Jupiter of all.)

[56]

Redeth his volumes / that ben large & wyde   [Leaf 10 a.]
Seueryly set / in sadnes of sentence   Read his large
                                                    volumes
Enlumyned with colours fressh on euery side 388
Me lacketh witte / I haue none eloquence   illuminated with
To gyue hym lawde / after his excellence   fresh colours.
For I dar saye / he lefte hym not a lyue
That coude his connyng / sufficiently discriue 392

      Ther to syng sanctus insessavntly   *Hill's Text.*]
384   Emonge the mvses nyne celestyall,
      Before the hyeste Iubyter of all.

¶ Redyth hys volumes that be large & wyde,
   Severyly sette in sadnes of sentence,
388   Enlumined with colovres fresshe on euery side.   [fl C lxiiij.]
   Me lakketh wytt, I haue non eloquence,
   To geve hym lawde after his excellence,
   ffor I dare saye he lefte hym not alyve
392   That covde his cunyng ssufficiently discryve.

[57]

But his werkys his laude moste nede conquere,
  He may neuer oute of remembrance die,
His werkys shall his [name[1]] conuey and bere 395 [1 MS. here repeats werkys.]
  Aboute the world all-most eternallie;
  Lette his owne werkys prayse hym and magnifie;
    I dare not preyse, for fere that I offende,
    My lewde langage shuld rather appeyre than amend.

[58]

Lo, my childe, thes good faders Auñcient
  Repide the feldis fresshe of fulsumnesse,
The floures feyre they gadderid vp and hent, 402
  Of siluereus langage the tresoure and richesse;
  Who wolle hit haue, my litle childe, doutelesse
    Must of hem begge, ther is no more to say,
    For of oure toung they were bothe locke and key.

[59]

There can no man there fames nowe disteyne,
  Thanbawmede toung and aureate sentence,
Men gette hit nowe by cantelmele, and gleyne 409
  Here and there wyth besy diligence,
  And fayne wolde riche the crafte of eloquence;
    But be the glaynes is hit often sene,
    In whois feldis they glayned haue and bene. 413

¶ But his werkes his lavde must nede conquere;   [Hit's Text.]
  thei may never owt of remembravnce dye;
  hys werkes shall his name conveye & bere
396 Abowte the world almoste eternelly.
  lete his owne werkis prayse hym, & magnyfye;
    I dare not prayse, leest for fere I offende;
    My langage shuld rathere apayere than amend.

¶ Loo, my child, this faders avncyente
401 Repen the fyldes ffresshe of fulsomnes;
  the flowres fresshe thei gadered vp, & hente.
  Off syluer langage the greate ryches

[57]

But his werkis / his laude / must nede co*nqu*ere		His works
They may neuer / out of remembraunce dye		
His werkis shal his name conueye & bere	395	shall bear his name about the world almost eternally.
Aboute the worlde / almost eternely		
Lete his owe*n* werkis preyse hym & magnefie		
I dar not preyse / for fere lest I offende		
My la*n*gage / shold rather apeyre than amende	399	

[58]

Loo my child*e* / these faders auncyente		[Leaf 10 b.] These ancient fathers reaped the fields,
Repen the feldes fresshe of fulsomnes		
The flours fresh they gadred vp & hente	402	and gathered the flowers.
Of siluer langage / the grete riches		He who wants silver words must beg of them.
Who wil it haue my lityl childe doutles		
Muste of hem begge / ther is no more to saye		
For of our tunge / they were both lok & kaye	406	

[59]

Ther can noma*n* now her werkis disteyne		
The enbamed tunge / and aureate sentence		
Men gete it now / by cantelmele & gleyne	409	Now we only glean,
Here and there by besy diligence		
And fayne wold reche / her craft of eloque*n*ce		and by the gleaning one sees in whose fields the gleaners have been.
And by the gleyne / it is ful oft sene		
In whos felde / the gleyners haue bene	413	

[*Hill's Text.*]

404	who wilt yt haue, my child, dowtles
	Muste of the*m* bege: there ys no more to saye,
	ffor of owre tonge *thei* were both loke & keye ;

	¶ Ther ca*n* no man *ther* werkes dysteyne :
408	The enbamed tonge & avreat sentence,
	Me*n* gete yt now by ca*n*telmele, & glene
	here & there by besy delygence,
	& fayne wold reche *ther* crafte of eloqvence ;
412	& by *the* gleyne ytt ys full ofte sene
	In whose fylde the gleners haue bene.

[60]

As vnto me Age hath bede good morowe,
I am not able clenly for to gleyne,
Nature is feyne of crafte here eien to borowe, 416
Me fayleth clerenesse of myn eien tweyne;
Begge I may, I can no gleyn certeyn,
Ther-for that werke I wolle playnly remytte
To folke yong, more persaunt clere of wytte. 420

[61]

And syke also, and in case ye fynde
Suche gleynes fresch as hath some apparence
Of fayre langage, yet take them and vnbynde, 423
And preueth what they beth in existence,
Coloured in langage, savory in sentence,
And dou[te]th not, my childe, wythoute drede,
Hit woll profite such thyng to se and rede. 427

[62]

Yit eft-sonnys, my childe, let vs resorte
To the intente of oure fyrst matiere
Digresside, somwhat fulle we wolld reporte, 430
And reuyue the lawde of them that were
Founders of oure langage, thilke fadyrs dere,
Who-is soulis god [aboue] in b[l]esse inhaunce
That lusten so oure langage to Avaunce. 434

¶ And vnto my age bot good morowe [*Hul's Text.*]
 I am not able clerly for to gleyne,
416 Nature ys fayne of crafte her eyen to borow;
 Me lakketh clernes of myne eyen twayne;
 Begge I may / gleyne I may not certeyne;
 *ther*fore *that* werke I will playnly remytte
420 To folk*is* yong, more passyng clere of wyte.

¶ Seche ye *ther*fore, & in caas ye fynde
 suche glenars fresshe as haue su*m* apparens
 Off fayer la*n*gage, yet take the*m*, & vnbynde,
424 & preve ye what *the*i be i*n* existence

[60]

And vnto me / age hath bode good morowe
I am not able clenly / for to gleyne — *I cannot glean,*
Nature is fayn of craft / her eyen to borowe 416
Me lacketh clerenes / of myn eyen tweyne
Begge I maye / gleyne I can not certeyne — *I can only beg:*
Therfore þᵗ werck / I wil playnly remytte — *gleaning I give up to younger folks.*
To folkis yong / more passyng clere of witte 420

[61]

Seche ye therfore / and in caas ye fynde — *If you find such gleaners,*
Such gleynors fressh as haue som apperence
Of fayr langage / yet take hem & vnbynde 423 *unbind their sheaves:*
And preue ye / what they be in existence
Colourd in langage / sauerly in sentence — *their fair speech*
And doubte not my childe / withoute drede
It wil prouffite to see suche thingis & red[e]¹ 427 *will profit you.*

[62]

Yet eft sones my childe / lete vs resorte — *[Leaf 11 a.] But let us return to our first subject.*
To thentente of yur first matere
Degressed somwhat / for we wold reporte 430
And reuiue the laude of hem that were
Famous in our langage / these faders dere
Whos sowles in blysse / god eternel auaunce
That lysten so our langage to enhaunce 434

¹ A hole in the paper.

[Hill's Text.]

  Colovred in langage, saverly in sentence,
  & dowte not, my child, with-owt drede
427 yt will profet to se such thyngis, & rede.

¶ Ye, efte-soones, my child, let vs resorte
  To the yntent of your fyrst matere
  Degressed somwhat, for we wolde reporte
  & revyue the lawde of them that were
432 famovs in owre langage, thise faders dere
  whos¹ sowles in blis, god eternall avaunce,
  that lysten sone owre langage to enhavnce!

¹ The *s* is by a later hand.

[63]

Than, litle childe, I councelle you that ye
Take hede vnto the norture that men vse,
Newe founden or Auncient whet[h]er hit be,　437
So shall no man youre curteyse refuse ;
The guise and custome shall you, my childe, excuse ;
Mennys werkys haue often entirchaunge,
That nowe is norture, sumtyme had ben full straunge.

[64]

Thinges whilome vside ben layde aside,
And new fetis dayly ben contryvyde,
Men[nys actes] can in no plight abyde,　444
They ben chaungeable and oft mevide,
Thing some-tyme alowide is nowe represide,
And aftir this shall thingis vppe aryse,
That men sette nowe but [at] litle a prise.　448

[65]

Thus mene I, my childe, that ye shull vse and haunte
The guise of them that don most manerly,
But be ware of vnthrefte ruskyn galaunte,　451
Counterfetoure vncunnyng of curtesie,
His tecches ben infecte wyth vilonye,
Vngerde, vnblesside, seruyng at the table,
Me semeth hym seruaunt full pendable.　455

[Hill's Text.]
[ff C lxiiij back.]

¶ Then litill Iohn, I consayle you that ye
436　Take hede to the nortvres that men vse,
newe fownd or avncyent, whether yt be ;
So shall no man your curtesye refuse ;
the gyse & custum, my child, shall you excuse.
440　Menys werkes haue oftyn enterchavnce ;
that now ys norture, somtyme hath be stravnge ;

¶ Thyngis whylom vsed be now layd a-syde,
& newe fetes dayly be contryved :
444　Menys actes can in no plyte abyde,
They be chavngable & ofte meved ;

[63]

Thenne lityl Iohn / I counceyl you that ye
Take hede to the norture / that men vse
Newe founde / or auncyent whether it be 437
So shal no man / your curtoisye refuse
The guyse & custom / my child shal you excuse
Mennys werkis / haue often encherchañge
That nowe is norture / somtyme had be strañge 441

Little Jack, take heed to the manners of your time,

for customs change,

[64]

Thingis whilom vsed / ben now leyd a syde
And newe feetis / dayly ben contreuide
Mennys actes / can in no plyte abyde 444
They be changeable ande ofte meuide
Thingis somtyme alowed / is now repreuid
And after this / shal thinges vp aryse
That men set now / but at lytyl pryse 448

new ways are invented every day,

and will be hereafter.

[65]

This mene I my childe / þᵗ ye shal haunte
The guyse of them / that do most manerly
But beware of vnthryft Ruskyn galañte 451
Counterfeter of vnconnyng curtoisye
His tacchis ben enfecte with vilonye
Vngyrte. vnblyssed. seruyng atte table
Me semeth hym a seruañt nothing able 455

[Leaf 11 b.] Imitate the well-mannered, and beware of ruskyn gallants

of bad habits, serving ungirt,

---

448   thynges sumtyme alowed be now repreved ;
   & after this shall thynges vp a-ryse
   that men sett now but at lytill pryse :

  ¶ This mene I, my child, that ye shall havnte
   the gyse of them that do most manerly ;
   but be ware of onthryft [1] ruskyn gallavnte,
452   Conterfetter [2] of vnconnyng curtessy,
   hys taches ben enfecte with vylonye ;
   Vngerte / vnblessed / servyng at table,
   Me semeth hym a servavnte no thyng able ;

[Hill's Text.]

[1] A later hand has added y.
[2] The r is by a later hand.

[66]

Wynter ne somer to his souerayne
  Chappron hardy no bonet lust avale,
For euery worde yeuyng his maister tweyne,   458
  Vaunparlere in euery mannes tale,
    Absolon wyth the disculede heres smalle ;
      Lyke to A presener of seint Malouse,
      A sonny bush myght cause hym to goo louse. 462

[67]

O I passe norture ! fy ! fy ! for schame !
  I shuld haue seide he myght go hauke and hunt,
For that schuld be A gentilmannys game,   465
  To suche disportis thes gentis folkys be wounte ;
    I seide to ferre, my langage was to blounte,
      But of this galaunte, loo ! loke a while & fele,
      He feccheth his compace whan he shall bowe or knele,

[68]

Braced so straytly th[at h]e [1] may not plie,   [1] MS. the.
  But gaderith hit in by maner of wyndlese,
And ȝif he wrenche aside or lytil wrye,   472
  His gere stonte all in pertous [2] case,   [2] *Read* perlous?
    The scho, the hose, the point, doublet, and lace ;
      And if ought breke, somme thinges [3] that ben badde   [3] *Read* tounges.
      Shall sey anon, 'a knaue hath broke a ladde.' 476

¶ Wynter & somer to his soverayne   [*Hill's Text.*]
457   Capron hardy, no bonet lyst to avayle,
    For euery worde geveyng his mayster twayne,
    avavntparler In euery manys tale,
460   Absolon with disheveld heres smale,
    lyke to a prysoner of saynt malowes,
    A sonny busshe able to the galowes.

¶ O ! I passe nortvre ! fy, fy, for sham !
464   I myght haue said he shuld go havke & honte,
    ffor *that* shuld be a gentylman[i]s game,
    To suche dysportis gentill folkis be wonte ;

[66]

Wynter and somer to his souereyne
Capron hardy / no bonet lyste to auale   *not doffing his cap to his master,*
For euery word / gyuing his maister tweyne   458
Auauntparler / in euery mannys tale   *forward in speech, rough-haired,*
Absolon with disheueld heeris smale
Lyke to a prysoner of seynt malowis   *and lousy-headed,*
A sonny busshe / able to go to the galowis   462

[67]

O I passe norture fy fy for shame   *(though it's hardly good manners to say so.)*
I myght haue said he shold go hauke & honte
For that shold be a gentilmans game   465
To such disportes / gentil folkes be wonte
I sayd to ferre / my langage was to blonte
But yet sir galante whan ye shal bowe or knele   *When he tries to kneel, he works round like a wheel,*
He goth by compace round as doth a whele   469

[68]

Braced so strayt / that he may not plye   *[Leaf 12 a.] being braced so tight that he can't bend. If he twists, a lace is like to crack.*
But gaderith it / by maner of a wyndelas
And he ought wrenche a syde / or a litil wrie   472
His geer stondeth thenne / in ful parlous caas
His sho / his hose / doblet / point & laas
And yf ought breke / somme tunges þ^t be bade
Wil mocke & saie / a knaue hath broke a lad   476

[Hill's Text.]

468   I sayd to ferre, my langage was but blonte ;
     but yet, sir gallavnt, whan ye shall bowe or knele
     he goth by compasse rovnd as doth a whele.

¶ Brased so streyte þat he may not plye,
   but gaderyth yt by manere of a wyndlas ;
472   & he awght wrench a-side, or a litill wrye,
   hys gere stondyth them in full parlovs caas,
   hys sho // his hose / doblet, poynt & laas ;
     & yff owght breke, sum tonges that be bade
476   will moke & say, "A knave hath broke a lade."

[69]

Lat galaunte go, I mene, recheles ruskyn;
  Take hede, my childe, to suche as ben cunnyng,
So shall ye wyrship best conquere and wynne,   479
  Enforsith you in all youre demenyng
    To sewe vertu, and[1] from foly declynyng;   *1 Omit* and
    And, my childe, that ye loue of honeste,
    Which is accordyng wyth humanyte.   483

[70]

That is, to you to vndirstond And knowe,
  That youre aray be manerly and resonable,
Not appeissh knawen[2] and to mowe,   486   *2 Sic.*
  I[n] nyse aray that is not couenable,
  Fetis founde be folkys vnprofitable,
    That maketh this worlde so pleynly transformate,
    That men semen almost effeminate.   490

[71]

Pley not Iakke mAlaperte, that is to sey,
  Be ware of presumpcioun, be ware of pride,
Take not the fyrst place, my childe, be no way,   493
  Till odir be sette manerly abyde,
  Presomcion is often sette asyde,
    And Avalith f[r]om his highe[3] de-gre,   *3 MS.* hight.
    And he sette vppe that hath humanite.   497

¶ Lete gallant go! I mene, recheles ruskyn: [*Hill's Text.*]
  Take hede my child to suche as be connyng,
  so shaƚƚ ye best worship conqvere & wynne;
480 Enforce you in aƚƚ your demenyng
    To folowe vertu, & fro foly declynnyng;
    & weyte weƚƚ that ye love honeste
    which ys accordyng vnto humanyte.

¶ That ys for you to vnderstond & knowe,
485 that your araye be manerly resonable,
  Not apysshe vnto moke ne to mowe;   [Ihu 1503 per
  To nyce araye that ys not commendable,   Richard hill ; ff
                                             C lxv]

[69]

Lete galante go / I mene recheles ruskyñ
Take hede my chyld to suche as be connyng
So shal ye best worship conquere & wynne 479
Enforce you in al your demenynge
To folowe vertu / & fro folye declynynge
And waite wel that ye loue honeste
Whiche is acordynge¹ vnto humanyte 483

Let Reckless Ruskyn go! You follow skilful men, virtue and honesty.

[70]

That is for you / to vnderstonde & knowe
That your araye / be manerly resonable
Not apysshe / on to mocken ne to mowe 486
To nyce araye / that is not commendable
Fetis newe founden² by foolis vnprouffitable
That make þe world so plainly transformate
That men semen almoste enfemynate 490

[Leaf 12 b.] Don't dress apishly or foppishly.

[71]

Playe not Iack malapert / that is to saye
Beware of presumpcion / beware of pryde³
Take not þe first place my child by the waye 493
Tyl other be sette / right manerly abyde
Presumptuous ben often set a syde.
Ande alleday aualyde / as men may see
And he is sette vp / that hath humylyte 497

Don't play Jack Malapert, that is, don't be presumptuous. Wait till others are seated.

¹ *Orig.* acrdynge. ² *Orig.* fonuden. ³ *Orig.* pryte.

---

488 ffetys, newe fonden by foolis vnprofytable,
    that make *the* worlde so playnly transformate
    that me*n* semen Almost enfemynate.

  ¶ Playe not Iacke maleperte, *that* ys to say,
492 be ware of presumpcion, be ware of pryde;
    take not *the* first place, my child, by *the* waye;
    till oder be sette, ryght manerly a-byde,
    presumtvous be ofte sette a-syde
496 & all day avaled, as men may see,
    & he ys sette vp *that* hath humylyte.

[Hill's Text.]

[72]

To ¹ cunnyng persones regarde ye take,
   Where ye be sette in right atentif wyse,
Connyng folke cunnyng folke shulde make,   500
   To theire goodnesse ye shalle make youre summise,
And as thei do, ye mosten deuyse ;
   For this, my childe, is as the gospell treue,
   Whoo wolle be cunnyng muste the cunnyng sewe.

¹ MS. The.

[73]

And o thing I charge you speciall[ie],
   To womanhode good kepe you take alway,
And them to serue loke that ye haue an eie,   507
   Ther comaundementis, my childe, loke ye obey,
Plesaunt wordis to them I warne you saye,
   And in all wyse do youre dilligence,
   To do them plesure, honoure, and reuerence.   511

[74]

As at this tyme this tretice shall suffice,
   Disposeth you to kepe in youre mynde
The doctrines whiche for you I deuyse,   514
   And douteth not, fulle welle ye shall hit fynde ;
To youre honoure enrolle hit vp and bynde
   .Ryght in youre brest, and in youre ryper age
   I shall wryten you here-of the surplusage.   518

¶ To connyng persones regarde ye take,   [Hill's Text.]
   wher ye be sette, right in ententyf wyse ;
500 Connyng folke connyng men shall make ;
   to ther connyng ye shall make your surmyse,
   & as thei do, ye must your selfe devyse ;
   ffor this, my child, ys as the gospell trewe,
504   ' who will be connyng, he must connyng sewe.'

¶ And on thyng I warne you specyally :
   to womanhede take awe alway,
   & them to serve loke ye haue an eye,
508   & ther comavndmentis that ye obeye ;

[72]

To connynde persoñs regarde ye take		Watch knowing folk, and
Where ye be sette / right in ententyf wyse		
Connyng folk / connyng men shal make	500	
To their connyng ye shal make your surmise		their skill.
And as they do / ye muste your self deuyse		
For this my childe / is as the gospel trewe		
Who wil be connyng / he must þe connyng sewe	504	

[73]

And one thing / I warne you specyally		Specially attend to women, and
To womanhede / take awe alweye		
And them to serue / loke ye haue an eye	507	
And theire commandementis that ye obeye		speak pleasant words to them.
Plesant wordes I auyse you to them seye		
And in alle wyse / do ye your diligence		
To do them plesure / and reuerence	511	

[74]

And at this tyme this tretye shal suffise		This is enough for the present. Mind you attend to it,
Dispose you / to kepe it in your mynde		
The doctrine whiche for you I deuyse	514	
And doubteth not / ful wel ye shal it finde		
To your honour / enrolle it vp and bynde		
Right in your breste / and at your riper age		and when you're older I'll write you the rest.
I shal wryte to you / herof the surplusage	518	

[Hill's Text.]

    Plesaunt wordis I avyse you to them saye,
      & in all wyse do ye your delygence
511   To do them plesyre and reverence.

¶ And at this tyme this treatise shall suffice;
    Do pose you to kepe it in your mynde,
  the doctryne which for you I devyse;
    & dowteth not, full well ye shall yt fynde
516   To your honowre; enrolle yt vp & bynde
    Right in your brest, & at your ryper age
    I shall write you here-of the surplusage.

[75]

Goo, litle childe, and who doth you Appose,
 Seying, youre quaire kepeth non accordaunce,
Tell [hym], as yite neyther of ryme ne prose   521
 Ye be experte ; pray hym of sufferaunce ;
 Childer must be of childly gouernaunce,
  And they must also entredet [1] be   [1] *Read* entreted
  Wyth esy thyng, [and not] of subtilte.   525

[76]

Youre lytil quaier summitteth euery where
 To coreccion and beneuolence,
But where enuie is, loke hit come not there,   528
 For eny thing kepith youre trety thense ;
 Enuie is full of frowarde reprehense,
  And howe to hurte liethe euere in awayte,
  Kepeth youre quaiere, that hit be not her baite.

EXPLICIT.

DOMINE, SALUUM FAC REGEM.

¶ Go, litill Iohn, & who doth you oppose,   [*Hill's Text.*]
520 sayenge your quayre, kepeth non accordavnce ;
 Tell hym as ȝet neythere in ryme ne prose
 ye ben experte ; pray hym of suffraunce.
 Chyldren [1] muste be of childy gouernavnce,   [1] MS. Clyldren.
524 & also thei muste entreted be
 With easy thynge, & not with subtilte.

[75]

Go lytyl Iohn / and who doth you appose
Sayng your quayer / kepe non accordance
Telle hym as yet / neyther in ryme ne prose   521
Ye ben expert / praye hym of suffrance
Chyldren muste be / of chyldly gouernance
And also they muste entretyde be
With esy thing / and not with subtylte   525

Whoever questions you, say you are not yet up in rime or prose.

[76]

Go lytil quayer / submytte you euery where
Vnder correction of benyuolence
And where enuye is / loke ye come not there   528
For ony thinge / kepe your tretye thens
Enuye is ful of froward reprehens
And how to hurte / lyeth euer in a wayte
Kepe your quayer / that it be not ther bayte   532

Little book, I submit you to correction: but go not where envy is.

Explicit the book of curtesye.

[Hill's Text.]

¶ Go, lytill quayer, submyte you euery where
    vnder correccion of benevolence;
528   & wher envy ys, loke you cum not there,
    ffor any thyng kepe your treatye thens;
    Envye ys full of froward reprehens,
    & how to hurte lyeth ever in a-wayte;
532   kepe your quayre that yt be not ther bayte.

    Here endyth A lytyll treatyse
    called the boke of curtesy or litill Iohan.

INDEX.

H. stands for Hill's MS. at the bottom of the pages, O. for the Oriel MS. on the even pages. Cot. is for Cotgrave's Dictionary.

Absolom with dissheveled hair, l. 460.

Amyse, l. 376, amice. Fr. *amict*, an Amict or Amice, part of a massing priest's habit. Cot. From L. *amicire*, to throw round; *am* and *jacere*. Mahn.

Annoy no man, l. 170.

Apayer, l. 399 H., appeyre, O., worsen, impair.

Apish, don't let your dress be, l. 486.

Appose, l. 519, question. *See* Oppose.

Avale, l. 457, lower, take off.

Ave Maria, say, l. 27, 77.

Avoyde, l. 271, emptying.

Austin, St, tells men how to behave at table, l. 158.

Author is old, l. 414-18.

Authors, the right ones to read, l. 323, 335, 351, 365, 393.

Bearing, men praised or blamed for their, l 153.

Belch not, l. 202.

Beware of ruskyn, l. 451.

Birds and beasts, don't throw stones at, l. 64.

Blow not in your drink, l. 190.

Brecheles, l. 300, without breeches, of flogging.

Breth, l. 203, wind.

Capron, H., chappron, O., l. 457. O. Fr. *Chaperon*, " habillement de tête." Roquefort. Provençal, *capayron*, from Lat. *caput*. Skeat. *Chaperon* .. any hood, bonnet . . . *Vn Chaperon fait à i'en veux*, A notable whipster or twigger; a good one I warrant her. Cotgrave. 'Capron hardy' must then be 'a bold or saucy young scamp.'

Cantelmele, l. 409, piecemeal: *cantel*, a corner, bit.

CHAUCER, read his works full of pleasance, l. 335-350.

Chere, l. 131, face, expression on it.

Childly, *adj.* l. 523, O., childy, H., fitted for children.

Children are like wax, l. 6.

Church, how to behave at, l. 71-98.

Clappe, l. 80, noise.

Claw not your visage, l. 194.

Comb your head, l. 36.

Communicative, be, l. 316.

INDEX.

Compace, l. 469. Fr. *compas*, a compasse, a circle, a round.

Constaunce, l. 102. Fr. *constance*, stabilitie, firmenesse. Cot.

Couenable, l. 487. Fr. *convenable*, apt, fit, meet for, beseeming, seemlie, &c. Cot.

Crede, say it, l. 77.

Cross yourself on rising, l. 25.

Cumpenable, l. 151. Fr. *compagnable*, companable, friendlie, sociable.

Cunning, (knowing) men, take heed to them, l. 478, l. 498-504.

Cup, soil not yours, l. 186.

Dancing, right for a child, l. 305.

Deprave, l. 157, backbite, run down. Fr. *despraver*, spoyle, marre, make crooked, wrest, wry to bad purposes. Cot.

Detraction, the vice of, l. 163.

Disauayle, l. 290, harm, damage.

Discreue, l. 392, describe.

Disculede, l. 460, O., dissheveled.

Disteyne, l. 407, stain, spot.

Dogs, don't irritate them, l. 67.

Dress, to be manerly, l. 47, 52; to be reasonable, l. 485.

Ears, clean yours, l. 37.

Entredet, l. 524, O., entretyde, H., taught.

Envy, keep clear of, l. 528.

Estate, l. 122, lord noble.

Exercyse, excersyf, l. 318, ? practised, able to handle a subject. Fr. *exercer*, to handle, manage. Cot.

Eye, cast not yours aside, l. 101.

Face, have no spots on it, l. 38.

Farsyone, l. 186, H., stuffing: *farse* (or *ferce*, l. 191), to stuff; *farsure*, stuffing. Cp. Chaucer's *ferthyng*, of the Prioress, *Prol. Cant. T.*, and the Oriel text.

Fetis, l. 443, O., fashions. Fr. *faict*, feat, pranke, part. Cot.

Fewe, l. 171, little, few words.

First place, don't take it, l. 493.

Follow virtue, l. 481.

Founders of our language; revive their praise, l. 431.

Fulsom, l. 257, ? full, satisfied; or helpful, A.S. *fylst*, help, assistance.

Fulsomnes, l. 401, fulness, plenty. 'Fulnesse or plente (fulsu*m*nesse, K. H. P.) *Habundancia, copia*.' Promptorium.

Games, play only at proper ones, l. 296.

Girdle, don't loose yours at table, l. 197.

Glaynes, l. 412, O., gleynes, l. 422, O., gleanings. Fr. *glane*, a gleaning; also the corne thats gleaned or left for the gleaner. Cot.

Gluttonous, don't be, l. 180.

Good cheer, make it serve for a scanty table, l. 253-5.

Gower's moral writings, read them, l. 323; and his *Confessio Amantis*, l. 325.

Halke, l. 124, generally means corner; A.S. *heal*, an angle, a corner; but another *heal* is a hall, place of entertainment, inn, which may be the meaning here.

Hands, wash yours, l. 43; wash 'em clean at table, l. 262-5.

Hanging, the servant that deserves it, st. 65, O.

Harping recommended, l. 304.

Head, don't scratch it at table, l. 194.

Holy water, l. 72.

Humanite, l. 497, Fr. *humanité*, courtesie, ciuilitie, gentlenesse. Cot.

Inhaunce, l. 433, put forward, up. Lat. *in antea*, Prov. *enansar*, to advance, exalt. Wedgwood.

Interrupt no man's talk, l. 275, 283.

Is, l. 386, O., his.

Iubiter, l. 371, 378, God.

Jangelynge, l. 80, chattering.

Kery, l. 369, κυριε, Lord, [have mercy upon us!]

Knife, don't put it near your face, l. 192.

Ladde, l. 476, O., lade, H., a thong of leather, a shoe-latchet. Halliwell.

Language, silver, is to be learnt only from our old poets, st. 58, l. 400-6.

Lewed (ignorant), he must be who will not learn, l. 21.

Lips, wipe yours before drinking, l. 186, 189.

Look men, you speak to, in the face, l. 99.

Louse, l. 462, catching lice.

Luting recommended, l. 302.

LYDGATE, John, my master, l. 365; read his volumes large and wide, l. 379.

Malapert, Jack, don't play, l. 491. Fr. *Müiere*, malapert, outrageous, ever doing one mischiefe or other. *Marmiton*, a saucie, malapert, or knauish fellow. Cot.

Malouse, l. 461, Malo's.

Manner & measure should guide you, l. 125.

Manners make man, l. 238.

Mass, help the priest at, l. 85.

Matins, our Lady's, l. 32.

Mouth, eat with it shut, l. 241.

Multiply talking, don't, l. 320.

Nails, clean yours, l. 44; don't pare them at table, l. 247.

Norture, l. 436, deportment, manners.

Nose, clean it, l. 39; don't pick it, l. 41.

OCKLYF; read his translation of *De Regimine Principum*, l, 351-64.

Oppose, l. 518, 'I oppose one, I make a tryall of his lernyng, or I laye a thyng to his charge, *ie appose*.' Palsgrave. See Towneley Mysteries, pp. 193-95. Way, in Promptorium. We may bi oure law examyne hym fyrst . . .
.. let me *oppose* hym . . .
T. Myst, p. 195.

Outrage, l. 278, outrageous, beyond bounds, too talkative. *See* Malapert.

Owers, l. 34, see *pryme*.

Pater noster, say yours, l. 26, 77.

Pendable, l. 455, O., Fr. *pendable*, hangable, that deserves hanging, thats fit to be hanged. Cot.

Poor table, men to be cheerful at, l. 258.

Presumption, beware of, l. 492.

Pride, beware of, l. 492.

Print your words in your mind before you speak them, l. 282.

Pryme & owers, l. 34. 'The *prime* and other *hours* are the services *Ad primam horam*, *Ad tertiam*, *Ad sextam*, and *Ad nonam*, found in the Primer, or layman's prayer-book. They are sometimes called the middle hours, as distinguished

INDEX. 57

from Matins and Vespers.' H. Bradshaw.

Quaire, l. 520, 526, 532, quire, pamphlet, treatise.

Ravenous, don't be, l. 176.
Read eloquent books, l. 310.
Rehersaylle, l. 288, rehearsal, repetition.
Repeat conversations, don't, l. 288.
Report (tale-telling) is the chief nurse of mischief, l. 135.
Reward, l. 127, look at, watch.
Rising, what to do on, l. 23.

Secret, keep what you hear, l. 134.
Sewe, l. 481, follow, pursue.
Silence, keep, l. 140; in hall, l. 204.
Siluerous, l. 403, O., silvern.
Singing lustily is good for a child, l. 304.
Speak fair to folks, l. 60.
Speaking, the conditions to be observed in, l. 143.
Spoon, don't put it in your dish or on the table, l. 267.
Surplusage, l. 518, rest, remainder.
Syttyng, l. 302, fit, suitable. 'Syttyng or convenyent—m. *asseant .. aduenant.*' Palsgrave.

Table, how to wait at, l. 113.

Tacches, l. 176, tache, l. 198; Fr. *tache*, a spot, staine, blemish. Cot.
Taches, H., teches, O., l. 453, manners.
Teeth, don't pick 'em with your knife, l. 248.
Terre, l. 67; *tar*, to set on, provoke; O. Fr. *atarier.* They have *terrid* thee to ire. Wiclif, Psalms. Sc. *tirr*, to snarl; quarrelsome, crabbed. Wedgwood.
Thewed, l. 20, mannered.
Towel, don't soil it, l. 263, 266.
Traverse, l. 242, change from side to side.
Trencher; keep yours clean, l. 269.
Trety, l. 529, treatise.
True as the gospel, l. 503.

Weyne, l. 166, A.S. *wanian*, to diminish, take away.
Wind, break not, up or down, l. 202.
Wise man, the; his marks of a youth likely to be bad, l. 104;— his counsel as to speaking, l. 137, 147.
Women, always take good heed to them, l. 506.
Wyndlese, l. 471, windlass.

Yanglers, l. 207, chatterers.
Ydellye, l. 315, idly.
Ynympariable, l. 380, unequalled, L. *par*, Fr. *pareil*, equal, like.

The manufacturer's authorised representative in the EU for product
safety is Oxford University Press España S.A. of El Parque Empresarial
San Fernando de Henares, Avenida de Castilla, 2 - 28830 Madrid
(www.oup.es/en or product.safety@oup.com). OUP España S.A. also acts
as importer into Spain of products made by the manufacturer.
Printed and bound by CPI Group (UK) Ltd, Croydon, CR0 4YY

22/04/2026

02094914-0007